Waking Up in Heaven

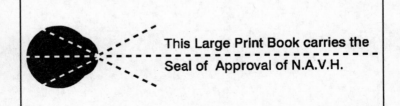

WAKING UP IN HEAVEN

A TRUE STORY OF BROKENNESS, HEAVEN, AND LIFE AGAIN

CRYSTAL MCVEA
AND ALEX TRESNIOWSKI

THORNDIKE PRESS
A part of Gale, Cengage Learning

GALE
CENGAGE Learning®

Detroit • New York • San Francisco • New Haven, Conn • Waterville, Maine • London

GALE
CENGAGE Learning®

LIBRARY OF CONGRESS CATALOGING-IN-PUBLICATION DATA

McVea, Crystal.
    Waking up in heaven : a true story of brokenness, heaven, and life again / by Crystal McVea and Alex Tresniowski. — Large print edition
        pages cm. — (Thorndike Press large print basic)
    ISBN 978-1-4104-6118-6 (hardcover) — ISBN 1-4104-6118-1 (hardcover)
    1. Heaven—Christianity—Miscellanea. 2. Near-death experiences—Religious aspects—Christianity. 3. McVea, Crystal. 4. Large type books. I. Tresniowski, Alex. II. Title.
    BT848.M38 2013b
    236'.2—dc23   2013013945

Published in 2013 by arrangement with Howard Books, a division of Simon & Schuster, Inc

Printed in the United States of America
1 2 3 4 5 6 7 17 16 15 14 13

I would like to dedicate this book to God. You found me in my darkest moments and changed me forever. I look forward to the day I will be in Your presence again, this time forever.

FOREWORD

In December 2011, I opened a Facebook message from someone I didn't know. "Laura, my name is Crystal," it began, "and I was compelled to write you after seeing you on 'The Dr. Phil Show.'" At the time I was promoting my new book, *An Invisible Thread,* which tells the story of my friendship with Maurice Mazyck — an eleven-year-old homeless panhandler when I met him in 1986, and still my good friend today. I was getting e-mails from many people who were moved by the book, but something about Crystal's message was different. "I, too, was given a second chance on December 10 of 2009," she explained. "That was the day I died."

It's not often you read a sentence like that, so I kept reading. I soon learned that Crystal McVea was a schoolteacher and a mother of four living in southwest Oklahoma. In 2009 she went into the hospital

7

with abdominal pain and suddenly stopped breathing. In the frantic minutes between when she died and when doctors were able to revive her, Crystal went to heaven and stood with God. Now, that by itself was intriguing to me, because I love hearing anything about heaven and what it would be like to stand face-to-face with God. But I was intrigued for another reason. Crystal's story reminded me of what happened to my mother.

When I was twenty-five my mother Marie's long battle with uterine cancer neared its end. She'd bravely fought it off for several years, until she just couldn't fight it anymore. Losing our mother was something none of us children could ever prepare for or even begin to comprehend.

On the very day I turned twenty-five, my mother asked me not to leave her alone. She said she felt strange and scared. I assured her someone would be with her every minute and through the night. The next morning she was unresponsive, and we called for an ambulance. Before it arrived my mother woke up and started weeping inconsolably. She was petrified and filled with sorrow, and she knew her life was ending. I'd never seen her like that, and I tried desperately to console her. I even told her she was only going to the hospital for a checkup.

"Promise me I will come home," my mother said to me.

Not knowing what else to say, I made that promise to her.

When she arrived in the ER at Memorial Sloan-Kettering in New York City, her oncologist examined her and suggested we have a priest come and give her last rites. My sister Annette and I said a prayer with the priest, while the doctor and a nurse waited just behind us. When the prayer was over, the doctor checked on my mother. He turned to us and said, "She is gone."

Annette and I hugged and cried and tried to find comfort in the belief that Mom was at peace, with God. That powerful belief sustains so many people in their darkest hours, and there in the ER it sustained us. Of course, we all yearn to know with certainty that our loved ones are in a better place, but that's not a gift we can ever expect to get. Certainly it is not a gift I ever imagined I'd receive.

But then, just a few minutes after the doctor declared my mother was dead, a nurse in the ER said something unimaginable: "Oh, my God, your mother is alive! Talk to her; talk to her!"

The nurse had seen my mother start to breathe again and open her eyes. We stood there in absolute amazement, and we looked at the oncologist, who was as shocked and baffled as we were. My mother had only occasionally been lucid in the previous weeks, but suddenly she seemed free of pain and in control of her mind and her body. Most remarkably, she had a warm, peaceful smile on her face, something we hadn't seen for the longest time. She was glowing, and she no longer seemed scared. Then she shocked us even more by speaking in a strong, clear voice. And what she said was this:

"I can't believe I've been given the time and the strength to tell you everything I always wanted to say to you but couldn't."

The next six hours were nothing short of a miracle. My mother's vital signs were inexplicably strong, and she was completely calm and in charge. She was moved to a private room, and one by one she spoke to all five of her children and her husband, my father, Nunzie, and gave us loving messages of hope and strength. "You have always been such a good daughter," my mother told me. "Laurie, I am so proud of you. I love you very much." Can you imagine what it feels like to have your mother tell you she loves you after you thought she was dead? Her doctors simply couldn't explain what happened — only our mother could. "I saw the other side," she told us. "It is far more beautiful and peaceful than we could ever imagine. I know now in my heart that I will be able to take care of all of you from there."

We asked the doctor if we could take my mother home. I'd made a promise to her, and, incredibly, I had a chance to keep it. The doctor didn't know what would happen next, but he let us check her out. Then came the final shock.

"I don't want to go home," my mother told us. "I want to stay here until it is time to go to my new home."

As much as we all wanted our mother to stay with us, God had a different plan for her. Still, He'd allowed her to come back and share a beautiful message with us — a message each of us would carry in our hearts for the rest of our lives.

Not much later, my mother sat up and told us God was calling her back. She asked us to all hold hands and say the Lord's Prayer and then leave her in peace. A minute or two later, she was in a coma. A few days after that she passed away at the age of forty-seven.

I immediately thought of my mother when I read Crystal's note, and I was surprised to learn that, while she had seen me on *Dr. Phil,* she hadn't actually read my book. She did not know my mother's story. She wrote me, because, as she absently watched *Dr. Phil* while folding laundry, she suddenly felt a strong urge to contact me. She'd felt the urge before, and she knew just what it was. It was God putting someone in her path. "I am just a mommy and a teacher," she explained, "but I know God is leading me to tell the whole story of what I experienced, and I would like your help."

I wrote back to Crystal, and eventually we spoke on the phone. She told me all about her time in heaven, and I was blown away. It is a beautiful story, not at all what I expected, and as soon as I heard it, I knew I wanted to help her in any way I could. I put her in touch with my cowriter, Alex Tresniowski, and he was just as moved as I was. With our help, Crystal got a literary agent and a contract with Howard Books, the publisher of *An Invisible Thread.*

Even today, I am amazed by the events that led to this book winding up in your hands. I am a retired advertising sales executive, and I was lucky enough to have some connections that helped me secure a publishing deal. But even with those connections I knew I was beating incredibly long odds by getting a book deal. So many people have inspiring life stories, but only a tiny fraction get the chance to share their stories with the world. I felt so blessed to have my book published, and even more blessed after it spent more than twenty weeks on the *New York Times* bestseller list. I have always known it was my mother in heaven who steered me toward Maurice on the corner of 56th Street and Broadway in Manhattan that fateful day in 1986, and I know she has had a hand in all the success that has followed for both Maurice and me. But I also know how very, very lucky I am.

Crystal, on the other hand, had no such connections. She didn't know a soul in the media, and she faced even longer odds than I did in getting her story published. In the months after she died, she spent a lot of time praying about the strange position she found herself in — while in heaven, God had instructed her to share her story with the world, but He didn't seem to give her any way to do it. She was a teacher, not a writer, and she had no clear path to anyone in the publishing industry. For months she wondered when God would finally send someone to help her tell her story. And for two years nothing happened.

Until, one afternoon, she saw Maurice and

me on television. She was only half-watching it while folding sheets and towels, but even so, she felt what she calls a "nudge," and she knew instantly she had to find a way to contact me. The idea seemed absurd to her — why would a complete stranger believe her far-fetched story, much less help her tell it? She prayed for days and tried to summon the nerve to message me. Finally, she brushed aside her fears and followed God's orders and contacted me. I could have ignored her e-mail or sent a cursory reply, but I didn't. My coauthor, Alex, could have been completely uninterested or busy with another project, but he wasn't. And the great folks at Howard Books could have shrugged at the idea, but instead they jumped on it. A million things could have gone wrong; instead, everything went right.

And that, I believe, was no accident.

The title of my book comes from an old proverb: "An invisible thread connects those who are destined to meet, regardless of time, place or circumstance. The thread may stretch or tangle. But it will never break." Just as Maurice and I are connected by an invisible thread, so, too, are Crystal and I. Our paths were meant to cross, and they did. Crystal hadn't read my book or known about my mother's experience, yet she

14

could hardly have found someone more receptive to her story. This, I now know, is the way God works — He brings people who need each other together. I refer to the unlikely bond between Maurice and me as an invisible thread, but I could also call it God's powerful hand at work. The long odds that Crystal beat in making this remarkable book happen are evidence of God's glorious presence here on Earth. And Crystal's story itself is evidence of the many gifts God bestows on us, if only we open our hearts to His many unplanned blessings.

I am extremely proud of the small role I played in helping Crystal, and I can't wait for you to turn this page and begin reading her story. I know you will be as moved and inspired as I was, and I believe Crystal's story has the power to change lives. We live in difficult and treacherous times, and the world needs as many positive messages as it can get. The powerful message of this book — that God exists and heaven is beautiful and each of our lives is its own miracle — is one that you will carry in your heart for the rest of your life.

Laura Schroff
Author of *An Invisible Thread*

INTRODUCTION

Someday soon, one of my precious three-year-old twins is going to ask me the question "Mommy, what happened to you when you died?"

Someday they will overhear me telling my story to someone and want to know more about it. They will look at me with their big, innocent eyes and try to make sense of what they're hearing. It isn't always easy explaining what happened even to adults, so how am I going to explain it to my kids?

There is so much I want to share with them, so much I want them to know. You see, my story is one of hope and forgiveness and salvation, and of the glorious healing power of God's presence. It's the story of what I saw and what I learned when, during a hospital stay, I left my body for nine minutes and went to heaven and stood before God. And it's the story of how, when I came back to Earth, my life was pro-

17

foundly and permanently changed — changed down to the very core of my being.

But it is also a story that, for the longest time, I didn't want to tell.

I live in a wonderful town in southern Oklahoma, in a community of friendly and God-fearing people, a place where passion for Jesus runs deep. Still, I know how much damage a juicy piece of gossip can cause. I was a teacher — someone parents trust to teach and care for their children — and I was afraid that if people heard my story, I'd be shunned and ridiculed and maybe even fired.

I was afraid people would think I was flat-out crazy.

And even though God's instructions to me could not have been any clearer — *"Tell them what you can remember"* — I struggled to understand why I had been chosen and what exactly He wanted me to do.

I struggled, because I'm the least likely person to be telling anyone about God.

Put simply, I'm not ever going to be on any short list for sainthood. Early in my life I was a sinner, and I'm pretty sure I broke every one of the Ten Commandments. That's right, not just some — all ten.

Even the big one — Thou shalt not kill. When I was younger, I committed a sin I

18

believed to be so grievous and so unforgivable, I was sure God could never love me, if He even existed at all.

And that was the other thing about me — when it came to God's existence, I was a skeptic. I had grown up in the heart of the Bible Belt, been baptized not once but four times, gone to church regularly, and heard a million sermons about God. And yet, deep in my heart, I wasn't convinced. Over and over I challenged God to prove He existed, and every time He did. I'd set up a new roadblock, a new challenge for Him to overcome.

I saw the hardships in my life as evidence that God had no interest in protecting me from harm. I questioned Him, and I cursed Him. And at times I vowed to cut Him out my life.

And still — *and still!* — God chased me and wooed me and loved me and chose me, and then He sent me back to this world to share a message.

And so, eventually, I began to tell my story. I told strangers in restaurants, customers at Walmart, and patrons eating ice cream at Braum's — anywhere and everywhere I felt God's familiar nudge.

"Excuse me," I'd say. "My name is Crystal McVea, and in 2009 I died and went to heaven."

How's that for an icebreaker?

And what happened after I started telling the full story of my journey to heaven is a remarkable, miraculous tale all its own.

Now I am sharing that story with you, in this book. Believe me, writing a book is not anything I ever thought I'd do. It's not like it was on my bucket list (like taking my kids to see a Broadway show and going to the Grand Canyon), and every single day I worked on this book was a day I had to pinch myself to make sure it was really happening.

But as soon as I got over my fears and started testifying, I knew that God's plan for me was to share what happened with as many people as I could. And frankly I can only spend so many hours a day at Walmart accosting strangers in the checkout line. Writing a book will leave me lots more time to get dinner ready for the kids.

Now, are there people out there who will think I'm a fraud, or a religious nut, or crazy? I'm sure there are. Maybe some people who pick up this book will toss it across the room midway through and write it off as fiction. *Who is this mom from Oklahoma who says she stood with God? Why should we believe anything she says?* One response I sometimes get is, "Oh, Crystal, I believe that *you* believe you saw God. I just don't know if I believe it." That's just a polite way of saying I'm either lying or crazy without actually having to say it.

The truth is, I know my story is hard for some people to believe. I know what I went through is beyond the realm of what we can experience on Earth. Listen, if someone had come up to me before this happened and told me they had died and stood with God, I'm pretty sure I would have been skeptical, too.

But I also know this book deals with the biggest and most important questions of them all: Does God exist? Is there a heaven? What is God's plan for us? Why are we even here?

I certainly don't pretend to have all the answers. In fact, I still have plenty of questions. Nor am I claiming to be anyone special. I'm a run-of-the-mill American mom living in the heartland. I spend my days begging my twins to take their naps, driving my older kids around to practices, and trying hard to eat better and lose a little weight (and not always succeeding). Before this happened I loved my life as a mother and a wife and a teacher, and that life fulfilled me deeply.

But what happened to me *did* happen, and now I know — after a lifetime of not knowing — that God *does* exist. He gloriously, beautifully, wonderfully exists.

And since God told me to share my whole story, that is what I'm doing — even though much of my story is painful and not always pretty. You will learn as you get deeper into this book that for most of my life I lived with terrible shame and horrible secrets. For the longest time I hated myself and believed I was worthless, and as a result I made so many bad choices.

But it's important to realize who I was in order to understand who I have become.

Some of what I describe about my time in heaven may be familiar to you from other accounts of people dying and coming back — the quality of the light, the shimmering entranceway, the presence of angels — but some of it probably isn't. Everything I describe is absolutely, 100 percent how I remember it — that has always been my one and only rule for sharing my testimony. Nothing is embellished or exaggerated even the tiniest bit. I always tell people, "If I was going to make this up, I'd have made it a lot more dramatic." What I describe is what I experienced, nothing more or less.

What I can say is that the things God

showed me were simply *astonishing* in their power and impact, and now the reality of God's presence bursts forth from my heart every day. The truth is, I was more alive in those nine minutes than I have ever been in all my years on this Earth.

And now I can only hope that through my descriptions, however inadequate they may be, you will feel even a fraction of the power and the impact and the absolute glory of what I experienced.

Not long ago I read about a national Pew survey that showed the number of young Americans who have doubts about the existence of God is growing. In 2007, only 17 percent of people aged thirty or younger said they had some doubt that God was real. In 2012, that number went up to 32 percent. That's roughly a third of young Americans surveyed who aren't sure if they believe God is real.

Then there is a recent comment from Professor Stephen Hawking, the famous Cambridge scientist. "There is no heaven or afterlife," he said in a 2012 interview. "That is a fairy story for people afraid of the dark."

Maybe the Pew poll and Hawking's comment should upset me, but they don't. And the reason they don't is because I used to be one of those doubters. I understand the skepticism, because a skeptical streak still runs through me. As a kid I questioned everything, and as an adult I'm still nosing around, searching for answers.

And while I no longer have any doubts about God and His power, I also realize that I am lucky, because I got to stand with Him. For many others, faith is about believing in a God they *can't* see. And for some, faith means believing in a God they have questions about. Just because you have questions doesn't mean you can't have faith.

My point is, I can't prove that what happened to me actually happened. Reading this book requires some measure of faith. Ultimately, what you take from my story depends on what you believe.

In the hallway of our home, just outside the bedroom where my youngest daughter plays with her purple stuffed donkey and my youngest son cooks up adventures for his little wooden robot, not far from where my oldest boy lifts weights and my teenage daughter texts her friends nonstop, a verse from the Bible is stenciled across the wall in black script. It reads

"Now faith is the substance of things hoped for,

And the evidence of things unseen."
Hebrews 11:1–3

Because of what happened to me, I know that God is real. But you don't have to die and stand with God to know what I know.

What makes God real for anyone is faith.

And so, when my twins come up to me and ask me about my story, what will I tell them? I guess I will sit them down and start by saying, "Children, there is a heaven, and heaven is beautiful."

CHAPTER ONE

It all started with a panic attack.

I'd had panic attacks in the past, and I knew what it felt like to have my lungs suddenly fail me. But what I experienced in December 2009 was worse. This was me gasping and choking and fighting to take in any air at all, and being unable to catch a single breath for a minute or longer. And the more I couldn't breathe, the more panicked I got, which made it even harder to catch my breath. It started happening more regularly, and a couple of times the attacks were so bad I had to be rushed to the hospital to get oxygen.

I went to see my doctor, and he sent me to an internal medicine specialist a couple of towns over from where I live in the dusty plains of southwest Oklahoma. I was thirty-three and in good health, though lately I'd been feeling stressed. The specialist took a chest X-ray and gave me an inhaler, but the attacks continued. The next step was an endoscopy, the little camera on a tube they slide down your throat to get a look at your esophagus and stomach. After that, they gave me something called an ERCP, which is a more serious test that pokes around in your bile ducts and pancreas.

The doctor discovered some kind of blockage in a duct between my pancreas and my liver and put in a stent — this little mesh tube — to fix it. It didn't have anything to do with my trouble breathing, but it was no big deal to fix it, so he did.

But when I woke up after the ERCP, I was in terrible pain.

This was a sharp, constant, excruciating pain, so bad I couldn't even move. The doctors ran a couple of quick tests and determined I had pancreatitis — an inflammation of the pancreas caused by the procedure to put in the stent. That, too, apparently, wasn't uncommon; any time you mess around with the pancreas or gallbladder, you run the risk of triggering pancreatitis. It's extremely painful, and the only way to treat it is to hydrate the patient and give them strong medicine for the pain.

The doctor told me I'd be in the hospital for a few days. Well, I'd had more than enough of hospitals — I'd recently spent ten weeks in one, the longest and hardest ten weeks of my life — so I told him, no, thanks, I'd be checking out. Whatever drugs he gave me worked well enough to make me think it was okay. Plus, I was just plain stubborn. I checked myself out against my doctor's recommendations.

That night I doubled over in pain, and I was back in the ER by dawn.

The doctors hooked me up to a saline IV to keep me hydrated and wheeled in a PCA — patient-controlled analgesia — which was a pain pump I could operate myself. It was loaded with several doses of Dilaudid, a really powerful painkiller. Whenever my pain got too bad, all I had to do was push a button, though it would only give me a small number of doses every hour.

That first day back in the hospital, I started feeling sicker and sicker. I was throwing up a lot and felt like I had a 110-degree fever. My mother, Connie, was with me, and she patiently wiped beads of sweat off my forehead and rubbed my favorite lotion — Noel Vanilla Bean — on my legs. But the pain I was feeling just got worse. The doctors told me I was okay. They kept saying what I was feeling was routine.

Sometime that afternoon, I got really groggy. I remember opening my eyes and

29

seeing my mother sitting in a chair at the foot of my bed watching TV. It was the *Bonnie Hunt Show,* which we both loved. Suddenly I asked my mom, "What year is it?"

"What year do you think it is?" she said.

"1984."

My mother laughed. "Well, honey, I'm in 2009, so you better come on back here."

Then I said, "I love you, Mom," and she said, "I love you, too." She went back to watching TV, and I closed my eyes to rest. As soon as I did, I felt an incredible heaviness, like I was sinking deeper and deeper into my pillow. I felt my pain go away, and I felt myself drift off into a bottomless sleep.

Down at the foot of the bed, my mother touched my leg and noticed it felt cold. She pulled my blanket over my feet, then got up to pull it tighter around my arms and shoulders. She saw that I was twitching, and she heard me let out a deep, unusual snore.

Then she glanced up at my face and saw my lips were blue.

My mother knew CPR, so the first thing she did was listen for my breathing. When she couldn't hear it, she put her finger on my carotid artery and felt for a pulse. She couldn't find that, either. She screamed, "I need a nurse in here!" and tried to lower the hospital bed so she could give me mouth-to-mouth, but she couldn't make the bed go down. A nurse came in and started a sternum rub, firmly massaging my chest with her knuckles while asking me, "Crystal, are you okay? Can you hear me?"

By then my face was turning blue, too — a deep, dark blue that was almost black. That snore my mother heard wasn't a snore at all — it was me taking my last breath.

"Can you hear me, Crystal?" the nurse kept asking. "Are you okay?" Finally my mother exploded.

"You can do that 'til pigs fly; it's not gonna work!" she screamed. "She's not breathing, and she has no pulse. *She's dying!*"

A senior nurse rushed in, but when she looked at my blue face, she froze. Then a hospital clerk came in and nearly dropped her clipboard when she saw me.

"My God, what's going on?!" she yelled.

"We have to call a Code Blue, but she has to be the one to call it," one of the nurses said, pointing at the senior nurse, who was still frozen.

"Call the code," the clerk screamed at her. *"Call the bleeping code!"*

The nurse finally called Code Blue — the most serious emergency code there is.

Someone barreled in with a crash cart, and someone else came in with an AMBU bag, which is used to manually pump oxygen into the lungs. A doctor ran in, then another, then a priest and a social worker. More than ten people pressed around my body in that small room. A nurse roughly ripped open my hospital gown.

Someone pounded on my chest. Still no breathing, no pulse. A nurse put a mask on my face and started squeezing the AMBU bag. People ran in and out and back in again. Other patients clustered in the hallway, trying to see who was dying. My mother spoke to me above the commotion, saying the same thing over and over: "Please don't go, Crystal," she said. "Please stay with us."

I did not hear her say it. I didn't feel the mask on my face or the pounding on my chest. I never saw all those doctors and nurses swarm into my room, never heard the frantic cry of "Code Blue."

I don't remember anything that happened in that room after I told my mother I loved her and closed my eyes and drifted off.

The next thing I remember is waking up in heaven, with God.

THE BRIGHTNESS

The very moment I closed my eyes on earth was the same moment I opened them in heaven. It happened in the same instant, which is how things are in heaven. Everything happens at once.

When I talk about it now, there's a sequence, because we can only understand things one at a time. This happens, then that happens. But that's not really how it was. Everything happened at once — yet with no sense of rush or urgency. In a way, it didn't even "happen" — my awareness of everything was instantaneous, as if it was ancient knowledge that had always been a part of me. It wasn't like I experienced something for a minute, then moved on to something else for two minutes. In heaven, there are no minutes or hours or days. In heaven, there is no such thing as "time."

Do events unfold differently in heaven? Or is it just the way we perceive them that is different? I don't know. But in heaven, everything happened in the blink of an eye.

The instant I came out of my deep sleep, I was aware I no longer had a physical body. I had left it behind. I was now in spirit form. I never examined my form, I was just aware of it — just like we know that we have ten toes without having to see them. My spirit form was not a form as we know it, with defined edges and shapes, but it was still very much a form, and I was very much a presence.

And even without a physical body I knew that I was still "me." The same me that had existed on Earth, the same me that had just told my mother I loved her before I died. At the same time, though, I had the stunning realization that I was the "me" that had existed for all of eternity, long before my time on Earth.

Unlike on Earth, where I was plagued by doubts and fears, in heaven there was nothing but absolute certainty about who I was. This was a far more complete representation of my spirit and my heart and my being than was ever possible on Earth, a far deeper self-awareness than the collection of hopes and fears and dreams and scars that defined me during my life. I was flooded with self-knowledge, and all the junk that cluttered my identity on Earth instantly fell away, revealing, for the first time ever, the real me. "Before I formed you in the womb, I knew you," God says in Jeremiah 1:5. And now I knew myself.

Imagine that — the first person we meet in heaven is ourselves.

The hardest thing for me is finding the words to fully describe what I experienced in heaven, because there are no human words that even come close. I grasp at words like "beautiful" and "brilliant" and "amazing," but they are wildly inadequate. What I experienced in heaven was so real and so lucid and so utterly intense, it made my experiences on Earth seem hazy and out of focus — as if heaven is the reality and life as we know it is just a dream. Everything I describe is as big and breathtaking as I make it sound — *only much, much more so.*

When I came out of my sleep, and realized I was in spirit form, I was also immersed in what I call a brightness.

Many people who describe dying talk about finding themselves in a pool of light, but that description doesn't cut it for me. For one thing, a pool suggests it was somehow confined, but in fact it was vast and endless, with no beginning and no end. For another, it wasn't just a light — or at least not light as we know it. It was closest to the color we call white, but a trillion times whiter than the whitest white you've ever seen or could imagine. It was brilliant and beaming and beautifully illuminating, and that's why I call it a brightness. In the words of the apostle John in Revelation 21:23: "The city does not need the sun or the moon to shine on it, for the glory of God gives it light, and the Lamb is its lamp."

But there was another dimension to it. There was also the sensation of cleanliness. It was a feeling of absolute purity and perfection, of something completely unblemished and un-broken, and being immersed in it filled me with the kind of peace and assurance I'd never known on Earth. It was like being bathed in love. It was a brightness I didn't just see, but felt. And it felt familiar, like something I remembered, or even recognized.

The best way to put it is this: I was home.

And so immediately I found myself in this otherworldly brightness, I realized I no longer had a body, and I became aware of the actual me — three incredible experiences you'd think might have blown my mind a bit. But in fact I just absorbed them without ever being con-scious of doing it, and they all made utterly perfect sense to me. So no matter how amaz-ing and mind-bending something was, I had no problem processing it. Not once was I ever confused by anything in heaven.

And that includes the other realization I had — the realization that I wasn't alone.

What I experienced next was the most pro-found and beautiful and miraculous experi-ence imaginable. My spirit still soars at the mere memory of what I discovered. God, in His infinite wisdom, gave me a gift that was so glorious, so perfect, I can hardly write about it without crying tears of joy. It was a gift that utterly transformed everything that came before it . . . and everything that would follow.

But to understand just how soul-shaking God's gift to me was — to appreciate the full power of what He showed me — you have to understand the terrible events that preceded it. You have to know the reasons why I struggled so much to believe that God loved me before you can appreciate the wonder and the glory of what He did to show me that He does.

CHAPTER TWO

I was five years old when my stepfather took me by the hand, led me into a dark room, and introduced me to Satan.

Maybe I'd misbehaved in some way, though I can't remember doing anything to deserve that kind of punishment. I guess I might have mouthed off to him or to my mom, which I did a lot as a kid. I was a sassy thing with a big mouth, and I know it wasn't easy to shut me up. Still isn't.

On that day, my stepfather told me he wanted to show me something and led me into the sewing room on the second floor of his mother's house. His mom lived in the same town as us, a small, flat place not too far from the Wichita Mountains. The sewing room was where she did all her knitting and crocheting, and whenever we visited, I wasn't allowed in it. So I was surprised that's where Hank took me. He closed the door behind us but didn't turn on the light;

the room was pitch-black. My stepdad got down on one knee and sat me across his leg. I could barely see him in the darkness.

"Crystal," he said, "do you believe in the devil?"

I didn't say anything — I didn't know what to say. For the past year I'd been riding on a bus that shuttled neighborhood kids to service at the local Baptist church, and I was just beginning to get steeped in the basics of the Bible. I knew that someone built an ark, someone was eaten by a whale, and a man named Jesus died on a cross. I also believed in Santa Claus, the Easter Bunny, and the Tooth Fairy, like most innocent kids my age. And, yes, I believed in Satan, though I didn't know much about him. All I knew was I didn't want to meet him, especially not in a dark room.

"I can call the devil to come deal with bad little girls," my stepfather said. "I'm gonna call him to come deal with you."

Then all of a sudden my stepfather yelled, "COME GET HER!" and shined a flashlight toward the back wall.

And there, in a flash of light, I saw him.

His face was a ghastly red, and big, pointy horns protruded from his head. His eyes were a terrifying white against the red, and his expression was hard and cruel. We locked eyes, and I screamed and jumped off my stepfather's leg. I tried to escape, but I couldn't find the door. I flailed in the darkness, and finally the door opened and light flooded the room. And there was my mother, Connie, coming to see what all the fuss was about.

I ran into her arms and held her tight. I remember my stepdad laughing and my mom scolding him and whisking me downstairs.

I'm sure I didn't sleep much that night, and the image of that awful red face was seared into my brain . . . and is seared there still. What I saw that night was something I never talked about with anyone, not even my mother.

It would be years before I'd set foot in that sewing room again. I was ten or eleven when my stepfather's mom sent me there to fetch something from her closet.

By then I was different. I no longer believed in everything a child believes in. I wasn't sure I believed in anything at all. Still, my heart thumped in my chest as I climbed the stairs, and I slowed down to a shuffle as I got near the room. Then I pushed open the door, ran to the closet, and dug around frantically for whatever it was I was looking for, desperate to find it and get out.

And then I saw something I recognized on the floor of the closet behind some shoes. Two familiar eyes staring back at me.

It was the bright red face I remembered from that night.

Instantly I knew it wasn't the devil. It was just a large, framed drawing of an old conquistador, his face painted red for battle, his helmet sprouting two horns.

I hadn't seen the devil after all. It had only been a stupid painting my stepdad used to scare me in order to amuse himself.

One of the terrible mysteries of my childhood had been solved, but even so I didn't feel any great sense of relief in that moment. If anything, I just felt more confused. I may not have seen the devil, but I was still afraid of him, even if I didn't know for sure if he was real. I was scared of a lot of things as a kid — scared of the dark, scared of empty rooms, scared of everything. Yes, I read my Bible, same as all the other children, but the scriptures were just words to me, and the Lord's message of love and protection wasn't really getting through.

I was taught that God loved me, and that He would save me, and that if I believed in His grace and power, the world couldn't hurt me.

But nothing in the little life I had led convinced me that was true.

When I said I like to talk a lot, I wasn't kidding. I've always been a questioner, curious about the world and eager to know why things are the way they are. As a child I talked so much and asked so many questions, my first-grade teacher had to come up with a plan to keep me quiet. She cut a piece of loose-leaf paper into five strips and handed them to me.

"Crystal, every time you want to say something, you have to give me one of the strips," she said. "When the last strip is gone, you can't talk anymore."

Not talk anymore? That would be torture. So I carefully managed my strips to make sure I didn't run out. But within fifteen minutes the first four strips were gone.

That's when I took out my scissors and cut the remaining strip into five new strips. I thought that was pretty clever, but my teacher didn't. She took away my strips and told me I had to be quiet for the rest of the day.

I don't know why I was such a talker. Maybe it's because, when I was born, I almost didn't make it. I was born a month prematurely in an emergency cesarian. My mom was in labor for twenty-four hours, and when a monitor showed my heart rate dropping, the doctors couldn't wait any longer. I came out weighing just 4 pounds 11 ounces, and my mother says I was an absurdly tiny thing. Even so, she tells me, I was adorable, like a little china doll with bright red hair and emerald green eyes. One of the nurses was so startled by my appearance, she told my mom, "You know, if that baby had been born a hundred years ago with that red hair and green eyes, she would have been burned at the stake."

My mom told her to be quiet and shooed her out of the room.

The doctors later told my mother I had what they called a failure to thrive, which meant I was barely surviving in my first few weeks on Earth. The problem wasn't only that I was undersized; it was that I came into the world wanting to do things my own way. I refused the bottle, and I was impossible to force-feed. The best my mom could do was feed me tiny bits of formula through a little straw. I was so thin and fragile, my skin hung loose like a baby sharpei's. The doctors may have called it failure to thrive; my mom calls it stubbornness.

I guess once I pulled through, I was just so excited to be alive I couldn't stop yammering about every little thing.

It seems that's a pattern in my life: almost die, pull through, then do a lot of talking.

When my mother finally got to take me home, she slept with me on her chest for the first six months. Sometimes when I cried I'd have trouble breathing or stop breathing altogether, and my mom would walk me around the room until I was calm and breathing again. My dad, who was thrilled to have a little daughter, tried to pitch in when he could, but my mom wouldn't let me out of her sight, not even for a minute. Finally a doctor told her to put me in another room, lock the door, and let me be. My mom refused. The doctor eventually convinced her to at least put me in a bassinet, which she pulled up tight against her bed.

I was so frail and tiny in those early months, my mother couldn't be sure I'd survive. One doctor was kind enough to stop by our house on his way home from work every night to check up on me. After a few months, my mother told him she appreciated his kindness, but there was no way she could pay him.

"Do you think I'd charge you to come see the prettiest red-haired baby in the world?" he told her.

My mother says now she never knew what it meant to truly love someone until she met me.

And because of that love, I finally began to thrive. I was still teeny tiny, but I was strong. I was walking by eight months. Around that time I said my first word — "Ma" — and I pretty much haven't stopped talking since.

Boy, did I love my mom and dad. I'm sure most kids think this, but I thought they were the most beautiful couple on the planet. My mother was so pretty, with her long, straight strawberry blond hair and the way she was always smiling and laughing and making everyone around her feel good. And my dad, to me, was the coolest guy I knew. Handsome, charming, confident, the life of any room he walked into. He always called me Sugar Bear, and I can't tell you how wonderful it felt that he had a special name for me.

I was also showered with love by my mother's mom, my Grandma Ernie. She was always visiting us in Oklahoma or having me stay with her in San Antonio, where she lived, and when we were together, she doted on me like I was her favorite thing in the world. We'd pick flowers in her lush garden or watch the cows graze near her property. I remember she had these bright, colorful muumuus she always wore, and I loved getting underneath them and hiding from the world.

"Has anyone seen Crystal?" my grandma would say, and I'd giggle beneath the muumuu.

Grandma Ernie was a beautiful piano player, and she taught local children to play on her upright Everett piano. Today, I have that wood-paneled Everett in the living room of my home. It's out of tune, but you can still play it. And whenever one of my kids does, I think about my Grandma Ernie and how much she loved me and how much I loved her.

Thank goodness I had my mom and my grandma, because growing up I didn't have a lot of other friends. In fact, for a spell, I had none. I guess my insistence on doing things my own way didn't sit well with the neighborhood kids. Early on my mom would invite other children to come over, but I was so bossy I'd never let them play with my toys. Instead, I made them sit there and watch me play with them. After a while they just stopped coming by.

My mom remembers one time, when I was three or four, that I insisted she dress me in my prettiest dress and do up my hair and even put a tiny bit of makeup on me, so that I could sit on our front porch and wait for a friend to come by. Mind you, I had no plans for a playdate; I just sat there *hoping* some kid would pass by and want to come in. My mom watched me on the porch, blowing dandelions and waiting for a friend who never came, and she said it broke her heart.

When I did get the chance to make new friends, I often messed it up. My mom enrolled me in a ballet class, and I couldn't have been more excited to go. I slipped on my little tutu and skipped all the way to the studio. Once I got there, I was fascinated by how sleek and shiny the wooden floor was, and a strange thought popped into my head — I wondered how many girls I could knock over if I threw myself across the floor like a bowling ball. I aimed myself at a group of five or six girls standing in the middle of the studio, got a good little run going, and slid across that floor with a smile on my face. I think I knocked at least four of them down . . . the first time.

After class, the ballet teacher kindly asked my mom not to bring me back.

I wasn't mean, just mischievous. For some reason I also believed I was on equal footing with all the adults in my life, so I was always asking questions and making suggestions and acting all grown up. I remember playing this board game I loved, Candy Land, with my Uncle Chris, who was in the Navy. It is a simple game where you draw colored cards and move your piece around the board on colored squares. Well, before Uncle Chris and I sat down to play, I stacked the deck. I set it up so that I'd get all the cards I needed to fly around the board and beat him easily. I was three years old, and back then I thought I was brilliant for devising such a scheme. My uncle didn't catch on for a while, but eventually he did. And when he did, he got up and stopped playing.

"You're a cheater," he told me, "and I'm not going to play with you anymore."

I was stung by what he said, but he was right — I was a little cheater.

I was also a kidnapper.

When I was five, I went to a day care center in the morning and kindergarten in the afternoon. One day we had a show-and-tell planned for kindergarten, and I got another one of my brilliant ideas. There was a girl in my day care, a little younger than me, who I really liked, and I figured I'd bring her with me to school. Not so she could watch the show-and-tell, but so she could *be* my show-and-tell. When it came time to get on the bus that shuttled us to kindergarten, I bundled her up and snuck her aboard. In class, I sat her next to me and waited for the show to begin. It didn't take long for the teacher to notice an extra little face, and she sent us to the principal, Mr. Booker.

"Who is this girl?" Mr. Booker asked.

I lied and said she was my cousin. I figured if they thought she was my cousin, they might let her stay. Mr. Booker called the day care and finally straightened everything out. I was sad, because the best show-and-tell ever was ruined.

That's just the way I was as a kid — curious, rascally, assertive. I had a lot of questions, and I wouldn't stop until I had the answers. I was always curious to find out what would happen if I did this or that. When I was three, one of the teachers at the day care sat me in a corner after I acted up. Unfortunately, she sat me right next to a light socket. This was back in the 1970s, long before socket guards. Naturally, I took off my red metal hair clip and stuck it in the socket. The electric jolt shot me ten feet backward. I looked down at my fingers, and they were black. The teacher got some ice, put it on my fingertips, and sat with me in a rocker until I calmed down.

But at least I learned what happens when you stick your hair clip in a socket.

Unfortunately, that's how I learned most lessons in my life — through really painful experiences.

The overriding memory I have of my early childhood, though, is of my parents' marriage falling apart. My dad, who was only twenty when they got married, was crazy in love with my mom, and their wedding in a local church was a joyous event. His brothers decked out his car with tin cans and shaving cream, and his pastor came down from Illinois to perform the ceremony. But the simple truth is they got married way too young, and they didn't realize they each had a lot of growing up to do. Before too long, the cracks started to show.

After the Air Force my father became a DJ at a local club and, by his own admission, allowed himself to get sucked into a life of parties and drinking. He worked six nights a week, and he wasn't around much, either for me or for my mom. And when he was around, my parents fought a lot.

Sadly, I have only one memory of my mother and father together, and that is of them fighting in our living room, screaming and shoving each other. I can't pull up a single other memory of them together during their marriage. My mother remembers that fight; my father says it never happened. That is pretty much the story of their breakup: two different sides, conflicting memories, and very little I could then — and even now — hold on to as the truth. They were both young, and they each made mistakes. And that, to me, is as good an explanation of what happened as there is.

What I do know is when my parents split up, my life changed drastically. Their divorce when I was three years old marks a very clear turning point for me. It is the moment, I believe, when I became vulnerable.

It is when the battle for my soul began.

My mother remarried within a year. My stepfather, Hank, was a diesel mechanic who grew up in the backwoods of eastern Oklahoma. He was a lean, hard man with a gruff auburn beard and shaggy red hair. At first I found him friendly and fun. He liked to sling me over his shoulder and call me his sack of potatoes. Or he'd have us make what he called family sandwiches. The two pieces of bread were my mom and Hank, and I was the cold cut in between. They would surround me in a big hug, and I'd squeal and say, "I'm the bologna!" Hank also got me my first dog, a scruffy little brown mutt he named Critter. I *adored* Critter. But my sweetest memory of Hank is when he took me to a carnival and carried me through the fun house. It was pitch-black, and monsters kept jumping out and scaring us. My mom said she could hear me *and* my stepdad screaming our lungs out, so loudly a carnie had to open a side door to let us out.

But then something terrible happened to Hank, and he became the monster.

Fooling me into thinking I'd seen Satan was not the worst thing he did to me once he joined the family, not by a long shot. One night, when I was five, he and my mother had a horrible fight, worse than any fight she'd ever had with my dad. Hank was drugged up or drunk or both, and when he got angry enough, he grabbed his rifle and made his way to my bedroom.

I was fast asleep in my sweet little room, with its yellow-checked curtains and matching bedspread, snuggled up with my best friend Snoozy, a giant teddy bear in red-and-white pajamas, slippers, and a nightcap that Hank had bought for me on my third birthday. I never heard the fighting or what happened next. With my mother running after him screaming for him to stop, Hank stood just inside my bedroom and aimed his gun at my bed.

Then he pulled the trigger.

The explosion stopped my mom in her tracks. Hank came out, the shotgun still smoking in his hands, and looked at her.

"There," he said, "I killed her."

CHAPTER THREE

The bullet missed my head by about a foot. It blew a big hole in the wall just above my headboard. Amazingly, I didn't even wake up. I never figured out if Hank deliberately shot over my head just to terrorize my mom — the same way he'd scared me with the devil painting — or if he missed because he was too drunk to shoot straight. Either way, it was another close call.

Hank wasn't always a monster. I clearly remember loving him, because he was there for me after my parents' difficult divorce. In the years after, I was desperate to see my father as much as I could — to still have him hold me and call me Sugar Bear. But that's not how it worked out. I wound up seeing my dad only a handful of times a year. The divorce gave him visitation rights, but there were lots of times when a planned visit just didn't happen. My mother remembers me getting dressed up and waiting on the porch for my dad to arrive, then shuffling back inside hours later, heartbroken. Then again, my father remembers showing up for scheduled visits and finding no one home. Conflicting memories, different versions, no way to know the truth.

Then, when I was four, my mother got pregnant again. My first reaction when my mom told me was indignation — I was upset she and Hank made a baby without involving me. I didn't know how babies were made — I figured it was like putting dough in an oven. All I knew is that it sounded fun, and I was mad they did it without me.

Naturally, I demanded my mother explain why they'd left me out. She knew I wouldn't stop bugging her until I had an answer, so she sat me down and explained the facts of life. Was I shocked! But the very next day I pulled all the other kids around me at day care and proudly described to them where babies come from. The teacher didn't much appreciate my little biology lecture, so she cut it short and ratted me out to my mom.

The truth is, I was just so excited by the idea of having a baby brother or sister. I remember my mom showing me her positive pregnancy test — I probably insisted on seeing it — and me being mesmerized by this strange little vial (this was way before test strips). I made her leave the vial on top of the television for weeks, because I thought it was the baby and I wanted to watch it grow.

There was only one problem with getting a sibling. Because there'd be a baby around the house, my dog, Critter, had to go. My mom and Hank kept telling me how great it would be to have a new baby and how Critter was going to a wonderful new home; reluctantly, I agreed to give her away.

I waited on the front porch with Critter the day her new owners came to get her. They were a young couple, and they said they lived in a big house with a beautiful backyard that Critter would love. They said that I could come see her any time I wanted. Then the man took Critter by the leash, led her into their car, and shut the door. And just like that, my only true friend was gone. For months afterward I asked my mom to take me to see her, but for whatever reason she never did.

I missed Critter badly, but even so, I couldn't wait until the baby arrived. Then, one morning when I was at day care, a teacher came up to me in the playground and said I had a phone call. No kid ever got a phone call, so I knew something was up. I ran all the way to the office and picked up the phone.

"Guess what, Crystal?" I heard my mom say. "You have a baby brother. You're a big sister now!"

The next day, Hank took me to the hospital to meet my new brother, Jayson. I remember being surprised by how tiny he was. Back at home my mom let me hold him, and I was instantly in love.

I watched over Jayson like a lioness. He had wild red hair, and he was a willful little firecracker, sweet as pie one minute and ornery the next. One time, I was pushing him on a baby swing in our backyard when a huge black dog ambled over from next door. This dog was bigger than both of us combined, and I was terrified. I tried to lift Jayson out of the swing, but his legs kept getting stuck. I looked back at the dog, who was getting closer and closer. Finally I panicked and ran inside, leaving Jayson bobbing in the swing as the giant animal approached.

"Mommy, Mommy, a big dog is going to eat Jayson!" I screamed. My mom ran outside, and I expected to see the baby swing empty and the big dog licking his lips. Instead the dog was gone, and Jayson was swinging and smiling away. I'm guessing he might have given that mutt a good kick in the chops. That was my brother for you — a tough little cookie.

When I was eight or nine, my mom let me start babysitting Jayson on my own. Most times it was fun — like when we watched the science show *Mr. Wizard* on TV, then tried to light a napkin on fire and burnt a watermelon-sized hole in the living room rug (well, it was fun until my mom got home). Other times Jayson knew just what to do to get under my skin. He loved riling me up and jumped at any chance to do it. If I had a friend over, Jayson would run around in his underwear, because he knew it made me crazy.

Yet no matter how much we fought, I always felt extremely protective of Jayson, almost like I was his second mother. And in many ways I was. As things got more complicated and chaotic in our family, Jayson and I were often left to fend for ourselves. And as more and more of the family craziness got dumped on us, I tried even harder to shield Jayson from it, even if it meant absorbing more of it myself.

But I was only a child, too, and I'd learn I couldn't always protect Jayson or myself from the harm that came our way. Like the big black dog that wandered into our yard, the evil that entered our lives was something I couldn't stop — it was only something I could try desperately to escape.

Just around the time Jayson was born, my stepfather Hank's younger brother Joe was murdered. I never got the full story, but I do know he was beaten to death in his own home. And I know that when it happened, it changed Hank profoundly. That was when he turned to drinking and drugs.

My mom's marriage became a nightmare of fighting and violence. But my mom was still very young and naïve, and she didn't realize what was causing Hank's sudden transformation. So she cut him break after break, and she tried hard to make the marriage work. She even got Hank to go to counseling with her, though it never made much difference.

By then Hank was like a runaway freight train, heading straight for a crash. He was sullen, withdrawn, wild, unpredictable. He constantly yelled at and badgered my mother, when he wasn't disappearing on benders and binges. One night Hank and my mom got in a vicious fight. I remember seeing her curled up on the ground, trying to block Hank's punches. I ran to her and threw myself on top of her to protect her, and as I lay there shielding her, the sheer terror of it all made me wet myself.

Then came the evening Hank nearly killed me in my bed.

After Hank shot at me, my mother rushed into my bedroom, scooped me up, threw little Jayson in his car seat, and drove us away from the house. At the time my father, Brad, was still living in town, and she went straight to his house to ask if we could stay there. Their marriage had ended badly, and they both held a lot of resentment toward each other. But this was an emergency, and my mom felt sure Brad would take us in.

"Crystal can stay here," my dad said, "but not you."

My mother refused to leave me, so she got back in the car and drove to her friend Bridget's home. I can only imagine how scared and vulnerable she must have felt to be turned away like that by my dad, but my mom just rolled with it and did what she had to do to protect her kids. In fact, I was still asleep in the car when all that happened, and my mother never even told me my dad turned us away. I only learned about it years later, in a talk with my father.

In hindsight, he says now, that decision is one of the biggest regrets of his life. But what I would come to realize is that he did what he did out of a deep well of pain. As a kid, I heard only my mom complain — and I only saw her pain — so I figured she was the only one who was hurt by the divorce. But my dad had been deeply hurt, too. After all, he'd lost his family.

I also learned that as soon as we left that night, my father got in his car and went looking for Hank. They knew each other and had once been friends, but on that night my dad wanted to kill him. Fortunately he didn't find him. If he had, life might have been much different for all of us — especially for my dad, who would probably still be in jail.

Hank's descent into madness created an atmosphere of chaos in our home. And in that atmosphere, bad things happened, and any chance to get them under control was lost. In the downward spiral of my mother's second marriage, bad things only got worse. The regular working order of a family — parents watching over their kids, weeding out bad values, asserting good ones — completely fell apart. And Jayson and I, still just children, became vulnerable to a host of predators.

CHAPTER FOUR

When I said that I had dark secrets in my life, this is what I meant. This is what I kept hidden for thirty years. It is very hard for me to talk about, and for most of my life I didn't share it with anyone, not even my mother. I just shoved it deeper and deeper behind a curtain of shame.

I was three years old when I was sexually abused for the first time. My mom left me with a babysitter in town, and the abuse happened there. I began having trouble going to the bathroom, and when my mom asked me about it, I told her something had happened at the babysitter's house. My mom took me to see a doctor, and the doctor confirmed that something severe had happened to me — something much worse than inappropriate touching. The doctor also said that because I was so little, I wouldn't remember anything and the best course of action was to not mention it to me at all. So my mom never brought it up and neither did I. She never took me back to that babysitter, but otherwise we never discussed it.

We wouldn't talk about it again for almost thirty years.

When I was five and a half, it happened again, in the home of a different babysitter. The babysitter had an older husband, and I remember him making me sit on his lap. I didn't want to do it, but I felt I had to. My brother, Jayson, was with me then, tucked away in his infant carrier. I remember looking at him sound asleep in his little carrier and thinking, *As long as I stay on his lap, he won't touch Jayson.*

This time, I didn't tell my mom about the molestation because I wanted to protect her from more bad news. Even at that age, I knew my mother had a hard life, what with Hank and money problems and all her other headaches. The last thing she needed was another crisis to deal with. So I never mentioned anything to her or anyone else.

But there was something else at work, too. The abuse was happening *again.* This wasn't the first person to do this to me, and I wondered, *What is wrong with* me? *How could I let this happen again?* I began to feel dirty and broken inside. That was another reason I couldn't bring myself to tell my mother — because it made me feel so bad about myself. For the first time I can remember in my life, I felt shame.

By the age of six, I'd already seen my mother's two marriages fall apart and endured horrible sexual abuse. So when I was put in harmful situations after that, I didn't even realize they were harmful. They were just my "normal." The reality of being sexually abused at a young age is that it identifies you — it becomes a part of who you are. It causes something inside of you to break, and once it's broken, it makes you vulnerable to even more abuse. That is what happened to me. All the shame and the dirtiness and the brokenness that I felt became my identity. This was who I was.

My mother didn't leave us with that second babysitter for long, but when I was six, she started taking us to visit Hank's mother once a week. Every Thursday night after my piano lesson she'd pick me up and take me to the two-floor condo where Hank's mom and his stepdad lived with their two teenage daughters. Even after she divorced Hank, she kept hanging out with his family. And Hank's family was, to put it mildly, really dysfunctional.

The ones who bore the brunt of it were the two daughters, Alice and Rita. As far as I could tell, their parents basically treated them as slaves. They were not allowed to have any friends or make any phone calls, and they had to come straight home from school every day. They spent their afternoons and evenings cooking and cleaning the house.

My mom would hang out with Hank's mom and stepdad upstairs while we all waited downstairs. Whenever the grown-ups needed something, they'd bang on the floor — once for Alice, twice for Rita. The girls had to run up, see what they wanted, and hurry back down to fetch it. I remember Alice and Rita constantly scurrying around with beers and food. It was obvious they were severely browbeaten, to the point of having their spirits completely crushed.

Besides poor Alice and Rita running around like servants, there were always people coming in and out of the house on the nights we were there. They'd go upstairs and join the party while Jayson and I stayed downstairs. In an atmosphere like that — weird, chaotic, toxic — a lot of bad things can happen to unsupervised children. Unfortunately, one of the worst things that can happen *did* happen — and it happened to me.

During my weekly visits I was sexually abused by someone in the house. It began as inappropriate physical touching, and it got a lot worse from there. It didn't happen every time we were there, but it happened a lot. And it happened for five straight years. I didn't tell a soul about what was going on: not my mother, not a friend, not anyone. For one thing, I didn't know *how* to tell anyone — just the thought of putting the words together and explaining it made me sick. But by then I was also convinced it was all my fault. If it had happened once, that would be one thing. But three times? With three different people?

I was the common denominator. The problem had to lie with me.

And where was God in all of this? Where was the Creator I had heard so much about? My mom took us to service and Sunday school each and every week — for a while to a Baptist church, and then to a Methodist one — and every week I heard about the greatness and glory of our Heavenly Father. But the concept of God as a loving father had no meaning for me.

You see, I couldn't fathom such a thing as

a loving and completely devoted father. My time with my own father was so very limited, and my stepdad was certainly no shining example of fatherly love. So when the pastors spoke of a loving father who would always protect me, it didn't make much sense to me. Nothing I heard in all those sermons and Bible classes seemed to apply to my life at all. And I sure as heck knew God hadn't protected me from harm. Just as my feelings of shame and worthlessness were taking root, so, too, were my doubts about the existence or goodness of God.

Now, Jesus Christ — that was a different story. Everything I heard about Jesus made him more and more attractive to me. For one thing he was human, not some celestial being. Plus, he died on a cross for our sins — he died trying to save *me.* After a while I felt like I loved Jesus, and I wanted to get closer to him. So when I was nine years old, I told my mom I wanted to be baptized.

I was in church when I first heard a pastor talk about how baptism cleans your soul, and the word *cleans* really stuck with me. I remember thinking, *That's what I want. I want to be clean.* So many bad things were happening to me, and the thought of having all the shame and the pain washed away with a simple dunk in the water was, for me, thrilling. I nudged my mom in church and told her I wanted to be baptized, and she took me down front. The congregation prayed over me, and that evening we came back for the baptism.

I went in a room and changed into a simple white cloth gown. The baptismal pool was high up in a balcony area, and it had a glass front so everyone in the church could see. I walked slowly toward the pool and could barely catch my breath. This was it! I was going to be cleaned! I stepped into the pool and waded in lukewarm water that came up to my chest. Then the pastor put his hand on my back and dunked me in the water, then brought me up and dunked me again. I came up dripping and spitting water. I had accepted Jesus Christ into my life.

And sure enough, I felt clean. I felt like my soul had been scrubbed. To this day, I can remember that feeling and how magical it was.

Unfortunately, the feeling didn't last. The baptism, I figured, didn't take. I assumed salvation meant being saved from all the crud that was happening to me; I didn't realize it meant Jesus was saving my soul. When all the things that made me feel dirty kept happening, I asked my mom if I could be baptized again. And so, a few months later, I was baptized again.

All in all, I was baptized four times: once in a Catholic Church when I was born, twice in the Baptist church, and finally in the Methodist church when I was twelve. And after each one, I truly felt cleansed.

But each time, the feeling didn't last.

And so I began to doubt if I could ever be saved — or if there was even a God in heaven to save me. After all, if God could save me, why hadn't He already? It seemed the path my life was taking was only leading me further way from God, not closer. No matter how much I wanted to feel like a loving child of God, I couldn't — I just felt unclean and unworthy.

But most of all, I felt like I was on my own. I felt like I had no protector, no hero, no champion. I truly believed that in a hostile world, I was all alone.

Looking back on my younger self now, it breaks my heart to think I felt so isolated and abandoned by God. I wish I could tell young Crystal not to feel so terrified and so alone, because — as I now understand — we are never alone, not even in our darkest hours. "For He will command his angels concerning you to guard you in all your ways" (Psalm 91:11). The truth is, I did have protectors, I did have heroes, and I wasn't on my own — none of us are.

God is with us always. And His angels are guarding us in all our ways.

THE ANGELS

I was instantly aware of two beings in front of me and to my left, and I knew right away who they were — they were angels.

But they weren't just any angels — they were *my* angels.

I recognized them immediately. There was so much brightness coming off them that I couldn't make out any features. But they weren't shapeless blobs; they definitely had a form, which was roughly that of a human body: long and slender. The being on the right appeared a bit bigger than the one on the left. They didn't move or hover or anything — they were just there.

And what I instantly felt for them was love.

A great, sweeping love for my angels overwhelmed me. It was like they were the best friends I could ever have, though the word *friend* doesn't come close to describing them. The angels were my protectors, my teachers, my mentors, my heroes, my strength, my spirit, my heart, everything, all rolled into one. I felt like they had been a part of my existence and my journey forever — as if they had been by my side for every tear I ever cried, every decision I had ever made, every day I ever felt lonely, not only on Earth but through all eternity. I felt so unbelievably safe and free in their presence, so happy and

fulfilled. I understood why they were there —
to greet me upon my arrival and guide me
back home. They were the best welcoming
committee you could ask for.

What's more, I realized there was instant
and complete communication between us.
What do I mean by that? Imagine a button
you can press; as soon as you press it, you
know everything there is to know about
someone, and they know everything about
you. Or a password that, if you let me use it,
gives me instant access to everything you've
ever said or thought or felt or written or
believed in your life: past, present, and future.
Instantly, I would have a more complete
understanding of you than is possible on
Earth. Well, that is what this was like — a
sensation that everything we were, everything
that mattered, was passing freely between my
angels and me, strengthening our profound
connection and an eternal bond. There was
no room whatsoever for secrets or shame or
misunderstanding or anything negative.

There was just this wonderful, beautiful,
nourishing sense of *knowing.*

I wish I could say I recognized them as
people I previously knew on Earth, but I didn't.
Many who have died describe seeing a favorite relative waiting for them in the beyond.
They talk about the amazing joy of such a

heavenly reunion. I would love to have been reunited with my precious Grandma Ernie, but I wasn't. I'm not saying that doesn't happen; it just wasn't part of my experience. Still, meeting my angels left me overflowing with joy. They never left my side, and I knew they never would.

In addition to my guardian angels, there was also a being on my right, and instantly I knew who this was, too. And I felt as if my spirit form just crumpled and fell before this being, as if — had I had a physical body — I'd fallen to my knees and raised my arms and bowed deeply in praise and worship.

Me! Crystal! The sinner and the skeptic, the one with all the questions!

Here in the presence of God.

CHAPTER FIVE

Please don't think my childhood was one long parade of misery — it really wasn't. Like I said, I didn't know what a normal childhood was, so my life seemed pretty normal to me. And I have a *ton* of really happy memories. Even on my worst days, I found something to laugh about. That's a trait I inherited from my mom, and it's something I believe helped all of us survive. No matter how dire things got, we found the humor in them and laughed instead of cried — like the night my mom decided to make homemade Christmas ornaments.

I was four or five, and she let me help roll the dough and cut it into the shapes of candy canes, reindeer, and snowmen. When we finished, she put them in the oven, and I went to bed. A couple of hours later, my mom rushed into my bedroom and woke me up.

"Come on," she said, "we have to go."

Turns out she had spray-painted the ornaments in the kitchen instead of the backyard, and in the process filled the house with noxious fumes. Even opening all the windows didn't help. So she and Hank roused me from bed, and the three of us sat on the front porch in the middle of a cold winter night until the fumes were gone.

That little bit of bad luck turned into one of my favorite childhood memories. After she led me to the porch, my mom dashed back in the house and returned carrying all my favorite board games. "Let's have a game party!" she suggested. I remember the three of us sitting on the porch steps — me in my pajamas and winter coat — and playing the game I loved most: Hook, Line and Stinker, in which you tried to hook these tiny fish with little magnetic fishing poles. I sat between Mom and Hank, and it felt like all the attention was on me. We played and laughed and joked *well* past my bedtime, and we forgot all about the fumes.

We make the best of bad situations — that's what we're good at.

When my mom finally divorced Hank after he fired his gun at me, we became a team of three — battered but still beautiful Connie; her sassy, smart-mouthed daughter; and her mischievous little boy. The years

75

when my mom was a single mother were lean and tough — we weren't dirt poor, but we were pretty darn poor. And yet, looking back on those years today makes me smile. Why? Because we found a way to make being poor seem like a big adventure.

My mother had gone to school to become a dental hygienist, and after the divorce she worked long hours for two dentists in town. She stretched her paychecks as far as they would go, but they never stretched very far. I remember she always served us what she called "poor man's spaghetti" for dinner — just spaghetti and sauce, no meatballs. It didn't dawn on me until I was much older that *we* were the poor men.

Mom tried to make all occasions feel special. The first day of school was always a big deal. Somehow she bought us new clothes and shoes before each fall semester, and she always let us pick out our own pencil cases and lunchboxes. If one of us got an award at school, no matter how small or silly it was, Mom was always there to see us collect it and cheer us on. If we played a shrub or a snowflake in a school play, my mom was there, front and center. When I was a Brownie from the first to fifth grades, my mom helped me sell tons of cookies. I remember our living room was literally jammed with stacked boxes of Girl Scout cookies, which we had to sort and deliver all over town. At the end of it I might have only gotten a tiny stuffed animal as a prize, but the true reward was all the time I spent with my mom in that cookie-crowded room.

I can recall so many small acts of kindness on her part. My mom packed our lunches for school every day, and every day she'd write me a little note on my napkin, saying she hoped I was having a great day or how she couldn't wait to see me again. Another big treat was going to the drive-in movies. Mom would make tons of popcorn and fill up a big brown grocery bag to bring with us. She'd spread out a blanket beside the car and let us kids lie on it by ourselves while she sat in a lawn chair behind us. I swear, I can still taste that salty popcorn, still see my brother's face lit up by the screen.

Even when I didn't deserve it, my mom was sweet to me. One summer she bought a small aboveground pool for the backyard, and she asked Jayson and me to help her set it up. Jayson, of course, got right to it. But it was a particularly hot day and I didn't feel much like helping, so I didn't. My mom said, "If you don't help, you don't swim."

Fine, I told her, I won't swim, and I sulked away.

Later I looked out the kitchen window and saw my mom and brother frolicking in the pool. They looked like they were having a blast. Clever kid that I was, I put on my bathing suit and stood near the pool, waiting until my mom felt sorry enough for me to let me in. I knew from experience she didn't always stick to her punishments. Sure enough, after a while, she let me into the pool. I'd been pretty bratty, but she still wanted me to have a fun day. I've never forgotten that one little loving gesture.

Memories come in different forms, some sunny and bright as a summer day, others much darker. And try as my mother did to help me hold on to my childhood as long as possible, the truth is, it was already slipping away.

I remember the first time I told God that I hated Him.

I was seven years old and in the second grade. There weren't a lot of places in the world where I felt safe, but there was one place where I *always* did — alongside Grandma Ernie.

Grandma Ernie was the only person in my life who always took my side. She was my champion and my biggest fan. I remember staying with her when I was young and wanting to watch a TV show in her living room. I asked her husband, a nice but gruff old guy named Jim (who I called Paw Paw) if I could watch. He said no; he was watching something else. Well, Grandma Ernie came in and chased Paw Paw into their bedroom where he had to watch his show on a tiny TV. And I got to watch my show on the big set.

But having the big TV all to myself suddenly didn't seem like fun. So I went into the bedroom and watched TV with Paw Paw.

Yes, Paw Paw was grumpy but he also made me laugh — and not always because he was trying to. I remember my grandparents taking me to the zoo and Paw Paw lecturing me about something in the parking lot. Just as he said, "Do you understand me, young lady?" a bird pooped right on top of his bald head. I laughed so hard I almost peed my pants. I also liked how Paw Paw was always falling asleep when he was supposed to be watching me. One summer Grandma Ernie got me my own kiddie pool, and Paw Paw's only job was to watch over me while I played in the pool on the back porch. Well, it wasn't long before Paw Paw was out cold, so I tiptoed into the house and got my grandma's bottle of bubble bath.

Soon, my kiddie pool was overflowing with bubbles. When Grandma Ernie came home and looked for me out the kitchen window, all she could see was a mountain of bubbles with my little head bobbing in the middle. My bubble-bath caper also led to the only argument I can ever remember my grandparents having. He wanted to dump the soapy pool water on the flowers so it wouldn't kill his grass, and Grandma wanted to dump it on the grass so it wouldn't kill her flowers. I don't remember who won, but I do remember Paw Paw dragging my deflated kiddie pool down the hallway and throwing it in the garbage.

In so many ways, Grandma Ernie made me feel protected and loved. It's funny looking back on all the little things I remember about her, like this pistachio pudding she always made for me, or how weird I thought she was for putting ice cubes in my milk. But to this day, the rich, nutty smell of pistachio pudding makes me feel comforted. Grandma Ernie also let me sleep between her and Paw Paw in their bed, which was actually two twin beds pushed together with a big sheet stretched across. I'd always end up slipping between the beds, and *that* was one of my favorite places to be — sunk down in the gap in my grandmother's bed, safe from the world.

But then I learned Grandma Ernie was sick.

I didn't understand much of what people were saying about her, other than that her heart was failing. She was only in her sixties, but she was a heavy smoker. I remember her getting thinner and frailer as the years went on. Then she wound up in the hospital. My mom drove us to San Antonio to visit her, but when we got there, it was too late to see her and we called her instead. I got on the phone and started telling Grandma about how exciting my day had been, but she said she was too tired to talk. I was surprised she didn't want to talk — Grandma Ernie was the one person who *never* stopped me from talking. She always said, "People who talk a lot usually have a lot of interesting things to say." My feelings were hurt, but I told her I'd see her first thing in the morning.

"Good night, Angel," she said. "I love you."

A few hours later, something woke me up in the middle of the night. I don't know what it was, except that it felt like someone shaking me. Only no one was there. I looked for my mom in her bed, but the bed was empty.

Instantly, I knew Grandma Ernie had died.

I went into the kitchen and saw my mom pacing the floor. Just then, the telephone rang, the loud rattle so much more jarring in the dead of night. I watched my mom pick up the phone, listen for a while, then crumple to her knees, shrieking and crying. "No, Daddy, no!" I heard her scream. I ran to her, and she grabbed me and drew me close. We sat there on the kitchen floor holding each other and crying. I was clinging to my mother as she was losing hers.

To this day I'm not sure how I knew Grandma Ernie had died before the phone call came. I like to think that maybe it was her, gently shaking me awake to tell me good-bye.

Not much later, I told God that I hated Him.

I know anger is only one of the five stages of grief, but boy, was I stuck on that stage for a long time. I was devastated by my grandmother's death and furious that a person who loved me unconditionally had been taken away. I remember telling God that I wished He'd taken anyone else instead. I know that sounds terrible, but back then, when I was seven, I couldn't process the loss of someone I cherished so much. It seemed like a horribly random act of cruelty directed squarely at me. Why did God have to take Grandma Ernie, of all people? Why would He do such a thing to me?

"I hate you," I told God that day. "I hate you, I hate you, I hate you."

Only many years later would I realize that — even in the darkest moments of my life, even when my belief in God was at its absolute lowest point — I never stopped speaking to Him. Our conversations may have been filled with nothing but questions and curses and doubts and demands, but they were still conversations. I vowed many times to cut God out of my life, and sometimes I did, but never for long.

For whatever reason, even when I didn't believe He was listening, I kept the channels open, and I had my talks with God.

Losing grandma Ernie made me grow up even faster. Her death just left me angry and confused. In time, after my grandfather got remarried, I surprised myself by becoming great friends with his new wife, Mary. She was spunky and funny, and I called her Gramcracker. We are still best friends thirty years later. But back when Grandma Ernie died, I was inconsolable. As I mentioned earlier, I'd always been a little precocious, talking to adults as if they were my equals, but when my grandma died, I had the real sense my childhood was ending.

Unfortunately, my situation at home only got tougher and tougher. Part of the problem was that I was so headstrong, which you've probably already figured out. I was stubborn even before I was born, refusing to come out for twenty-four hours, until doctors had to come in and get me. As a young child I resisted my mother's every effort to turn me into a pretty little girl — instead I was a defiant tomboy, never letting her touch my hair or put me in frilly dresses, except on Easter and when I dressed up for my imaginary playdate. All the other girls showed up for first grade in cute, colorful outfits; I wore a flannel shirt and jeans. And in the first grade alone, I got paddled by the teacher three times: once for wetting my hair in the sink on a hot day and the other two times — big surprise — for talking too much.

But even though I was difficult, I really don't think I was all that much of a bad girl. I did really well in school, usually As and Bs. Of course it didn't hurt that my dad — who was otherwise not involved with my schooling — agreed to pay me two dollars for every A I got. I remember how proud I was when I got to call my dad and tell him how much he owed me. He joked and told me I was going to make him go broke. But I knew he was proud of me, and I really loved that feeling.

So while I could be a little bossy and bratty — and often disobedient — I wasn't what anyone would call a problem child. I wasn't a *bad girl.*

But then once Hank came into the picture, and in the years after he left, that slowly began to change.

Looking back, I think I had some pretty good reasons to be angry at the world. My father, whom I adored, wasn't around much, and there were long stretches when I didn't hear from him at all. I remember my fifth-grade teacher asking me about my parents. I started crying and told her I hadn't spoken with my dad in five months. She seemed surprised, but by then I already knew that not having a full-time dad was just going to be a fact of life for me.

Then there were the years my mother calls her "wild phase." After she divorced Hank, she was still young and pretty, and she began dating quite a bit. I don't remember a lot about the men she dated, except that I grew attached to some of them only to have them vanish from my life after a short while.

During those years, when my mom didn't have a consistent partner in her life, she wound up confiding a lot of things in me. I knew exactly how poor we were, exactly which bills weren't getting paid, exactly how bleak our future looked. She also bad-mouthed my dad from time to time, telling me things I had no way of confirming. It was way too much information to be sharing with a child.

And in that way I became a coparent. Around the time Hank left, my mom pretty much made me Jayson's permanent baby-sitter, so I spent many nights taking care of my brother while my mom was out sowing her oats. I'd bathe Jayson and clean the house and sometimes get dinner ready. I became my mother's partner, not her daughter.

And yet I didn't begrudge my mother for doing this to me, because I believed it was my responsibility to make *her* life better. I knew she worked hard all day at the dentists' office, and I knew money was tight. And I knew she was lonely. So I tried my best to lighten her load, to make her happy however I could. I didn't want my mother to feel lonely and afraid.

But then abruptly, when I was ten years old, my mother stopped dating. All of a sudden, she decided she wanted to be a better parent. After three years of nonstop partying, she began staying home and making new rules and setting boundaries where before there had been none.

As you might guess, that didn't sit too well with me. I was angry and resentful about everything I'd had to endure — everything I hadn't been protected from. I felt it was way too late for my mom to get all protective.

By then I'd learned that in order to survive, I had to fend for myself. I loved my mom but felt I had no one I could truly depend on but myself. The abuse was still going on in Hank's mother's house, and there was no one I could talk to about it — certainly not my mother, whose burdens I was trying to lighten, not make heavier. I was on my own, taking on more and more responsibility, losing more and more of any innocence I had left until there was none left at all. At age ten, I was already a grown-up.

And so when my mom tried to become a parent to me again, I fought her tooth and nail. Anything she told me to do, I did the opposite. Any attempt to discipline me was met with screams and defiance. We fought constantly about everything — cleaning my room, watching TV, doing my homework; you name it. She'd taken from me my chance to be a regular kid because of all the adult problems she'd unloaded on me, and I sure wasn't about to start being a kid now. And I hadn't survived so many bad things as a child just to be thrust right back into childhood again. As far as I was concerned, my childhood was over, and nothing was going to change that.

The next couple of years were a nightmare for us both. My mother would order me to do something; I'd refuse and talk back to her. She'd push me; I'd push her back. Before long we were having real knockdown fights — wrestling with each other on the living room floor while a horrified Jayson looked on. Occasionally my mom would try to discipline us by spanking us or hitting us with a wooden spoon or a belt. But those punishments would only enrage me, and I'd strike back with all my might. When I was twelve, we got into a particularly nasty fight. I don't remember if she was trying to spank me with a hairbrush or what, but I do remember that I pushed her really hard. She pushed me back, and I toppled through a shower door and into the bathtub.

For me, that fight — on top of everything that was happening at Hank's mother's house — was more than I could handle. The next day I took what little money I'd saved from babysitting neighborhood kids and told my mom I wanted to buy her lunch at Braum's. We had sandwiches and ice cream, and when it was over, I told my mother what I'd come to say. She listened to me, then lowered her head and broke down into tears.

I'd told my mother I was leaving home. And that's just what I did.

CHAPTER SIX

I wasn't planning on hitchhiking to California or hopping a freight train or anything like that. What I told my mom that day was that I wanted to go live with my father in Illinois.

My mother, to say the least, was heartbroken. She was the one who'd stayed with me and raised me and clothed and fed me while my dad was out of the picture, and here I was telling her I'd prefer to live with him. I suppose she could have put up a fight and refused to let me go, but she probably knew that was a fight she couldn't win. I had made up my mind. I was going.

Luckily for me, my dad agreed to take me in. Shortly before I was set to leave, my mom threw me a going-away party at the local skating rink. There were balloons and signs, and all my friends showed up to say good-bye. A couple of days later, my dad drove all the way down from Illinois to pick me up. I don't remember if I cried when I left my mom that day, but I know for sure that she did. The truth is, there was no one closer to me in the world than my mother. And many years later I would realize she was the *only* person in my life who never abandoned me. She was my best friend, yet she was also my worst enemy. She wasn't a perfect mother, but she loved me and it was killing her to let me go. But I think she also realized this was the way it had to be. So I packed up my things, including my beloved teddy bear Snoozy, got in my dad's car, and left my mom.

Growing up, my dad wasn't poor, but his family didn't do much better than scrape by. He remembers always being aware of all the things other kids in the neighborhood had that he and his brothers didn't. He made a vow that when he grew up, he'd work tirelessly to give his children all the things he never had.

And that included the one thing he craved most of all from his own parents: attention. Odel and Mardel were strict Catholics who loved their children dearly, but they didn't always show it, or perhaps didn't really know how. So my dad's plan was to give his kids the attention and approval he didn't always receive as a child. Unfortunately, life got in the way of that plan.

When I showed up to live with him, my dad did his best to make me feel at home. He set up a room for me with pink curtains, a nightstand and clock, and a desk for doing homework on. He seemed very happy to see me and to have the chance to finally get to know me, but as the days passed, I could see he found it hard to show any emotion around me. That was quite a change from living with my mother. While my mom had an unpredictable temperament, kind and caring one minute and angry and screaming the next, my father was always the same — cool and distant. I was used to my mom yelling and cursing and letting *all* her emotions out, good and bad, and suddenly I had a parent who barely showed any at all. For much of the time, my dad was just a shadow presence in my life.

My father was in the nightclub business, and that pretty much took up all his time. Back in our hometown, after he and my mom divorced, he opened a little honky-tonk on the outskirts of town, and the few times I got to see him, he was always driving a cool car with a gorgeous girlfriend in tow. People gravitated toward him, and from what I could gather, he was the life of the party. In Illinois, he'd opened a nightclub, and running it kept him busy seven nights a week. Unfortunately, that put us on completely different schedules. On weekends I'd go with him to help clean up the club, because it was a way for me to spend some time with him. But, for the most part, I was on my own.

Still, I jumped right into my new life, joining the cheerleading squad at my new school and making friends in my seventh-grade class. For a while everything worked out fine, and my dad did his very best to be a real father to me. He'd turn up at some of my cheerleader meetings, or he'd drive me and my friends to games and even take us out for ice cream or to Burger King afterward. I remember my father bringing me to a school mother-daughter banquet and him being the only dad there. Once, when I was at school, I had a little female emergency. Normally I'd have called my mom, and she'd have discreetly shown up and brought me what I needed. But this time I had to ask my dad. A short while later, a school administrator called me to her office. I walked in, and on her desk I saw a giant brown paper bag stuffed with boxes and boxes of every conceivable feminine hygiene product ever made. The administrator noticed my horror and let me keep the bag in her office rather than having to tote it around.

Later that day when I got home, my father looked at me and said, "Please don't ever make me buy that stuff again."

"Don't worry," I said, "I won't."

If there was an emergency, my father would spring into action — like the time I tried to make my bangs look really poufy and dropped a curling iron into my eye, burning my eyeball; my dad rushed me to an optometrist, who gave me a cool eye patch to wear. Or the time I tried to cook him bacon one morning and burnt it so badly, the fire alarm went off, and my dad rushed down and slipped on the stairs, tumbling all the way to the floor. I just stood their holding my spatula, horrified, though we both laugh about it today.

The problem was, I didn't see my dad nearly as much as I wanted to. Out of all the birthdays I had as a child and a teenager, I can only remember him being with me for two of them. And I can't remember us ever sitting down and having a serious talk. And you know how much I like to talk. As a result, I had no one to confide in about my fears and insecurities and the gnawing sense of self-hatred I had always felt.

No one, that is, except God.

It was during the time I lived with my dad that I first developed what I would call a good prayer life. My mom had made me say my prayers every night, and long after I stopped listening to her I kept on praying. And when I was with my dad, I prayed even more. Mind you, I didn't suddenly start believing that God was real, and even if He was, I still didn't think He was listening to me. But because I was alone most of the time — and because, as I might have mentioned, I really like to talk — I found myself talking to God just about every night. I prayed for the homeless, I prayed for my family, I prayed about boys. As a teen I suffered from horrible acne, so I prayed a lot about that. I asked God to fix everything that was broken in my life.

The acne, for one thing, wasn't getting fixed, so I begged my dad to take me to a doctor to get acne medicine. But for whatever reason, he didn't. Some school nights he'd come home from the club at 2:00 a.m., and I'd be waiting for him so I could plead my case. He just kept saying he didn't have the money. So I woke up each day looking — and feeling — worse.

I decided to step up my prayers to God. They became simple and specific — I asked

95

Him to please make my father take me to a doctor. Night after night, week after week, I prayed. But, to my dismay, nothing changed. I concluded that if God was real, He wasn't interested in my problems.

When you're a teenager, your feelings are magnified, so if you're feeling alone and damaged, you can really start to think of life as hopeless. And that's what happened to me. I'd run away from home to escape the abuse, but when I lay in bed and closed my eyes, I could still see it all happening plain as day. I went from one parent whom I fought with constantly to another who was never around. At school, kids were making fun of me because of my acne, yet I had no way of making it go away. I felt like I had no control over anything in my life — like I was powerless to stop all these things from happening to me. Not even God, who I prayed to so hard, could help me escape my life.

And so after a while I decided the only way to escape it was to leave it.

One particularly miserable night, when my father was away at work and I was home alone, I went into his bathroom and opened the mirrored door of his medicine cabinet. I grabbed several bottles off the narrow glass shelves and poured a few pills from each of them onto his bed. Then I went to his liquor cabinet and came back with a quart of vodka. I swallowed all the pills and washed them down with two big swigs of vodka. For some reason I carefully refilled the bottle with water so my dad wouldn't see the missing booze — as if that would be the first thing he'd notice when he came home.

After taking the pills I sat on the carpeted stairs and waited. Suddenly I felt scared, and I curled into a ball and started crying and whimpering, "Oh God, oh God." Still, I didn't regret what I'd done. More than anything, I just wanted the pain and the sadness to be over. I was a broken girl, and there was no way to fix me. This was the only way I knew to make it all stop. It wasn't so much that I wanted to escape life. It's that I wanted to escape me.

And so I went to bed and closed my eyes and let sleep take me away.

When I woke up, it was morning and I was still around. Other than feeling really queasy, nothing was different. My dad had come home and found nothing out of the ordinary — not the emptier pill bottles, not the watered-down vodka (well, he did notice the vodka, but only weeks later after a guest complained his drink had no taste). I didn't really think too much about what I'd done and why it didn't work. I just sighed and picked up where I'd left off, resuming my miserable life.

It wasn't too much later that my mother came up to Illinois for my eighth-grade graduation. When she saw my face covered with acne, I could tell she was shocked. I'm sure she could also see that my spirit, which in her experience was impossible to suppress, had been all but crushed. My mother glared at my dad and did what she always did in times of conflict — she yelled.

"I trusted you to take care of her!" she berated my dad. "Look what you've done!" It was just another fight with my mom on one side and my dad on the other, and me in the middle not knowing whose side to be on.

But that fight made me realize one important thing — I missed my mom. I might have felt grown up, but the truth is, I wasn't. I needed my mother's hands-on attention more than I knew. My mom looked at me and said, "I need to take you home right now." Without hesitation, I agreed.

And so I went back to Oklahoma to live with my mother after two years with my father, and for the first time in a long time I felt optimistic. I believed that things would be different between us — that my mom and I were finally going to get along. After all, I needed her, and she needed me. We both knew that now. We were a team again, us against the world, looking out for each other.

Sure enough, the first thing my mother did was take me to a dermatologist, and my acne disappeared.

At the time, I didn't see God's hand in anything that was happening. I didn't give Him credit for my father's taking me in and stopping the cycle of sexual abuse in my life, or my mother's coming to get me just when I needed her most, because I didn't yet realize God sometimes puts people in your path to help answer your prayers. And I didn't wonder why I survived after swallowing all those pills. I guess I just chalked it up to dumb luck. Looking back, I'm sure that in the chaos of pulling down pill bottles, I grabbed a lot of fairly harmless stuff, like aspirin and who knows what else. But looking back, I also know it wasn't dumb luck.

It was God glorifying Himself through the garbage of my life. It was God chasing me down in one of my bleakest moments — something that He would do time and time again. It was God taking the very things the enemy used to try to destroy me — anger, bitterness, self-hatred — and instead saving me and showing me He is real. Only many years later would I realize that the God I worship now had found me in my darkness. And it was in the darkness that was to come that I would finally see His light.

Before long I would need God's help again, and this time more than ever. Because no sooner had I come back to live with my mom, she brought a monster from my past back into my life.

Within days of my return, my mother began seeing Hank again. The story I heard was that she was at church one day, and Hank came by and slipped her a note. The note said, "I love you and I love my children, and I want you all with me." So she took Hank back.

This was a devastating blow for me. The man who fired a gun over my head and beat my mom bloody was suddenly taking my little brother to school and hanging around the house again as if nothing had ever happened. Even worse, because my mother wanted us to be one big happy family, she decided to become a strict parent again. My defiant streak flared back up. The old push-and-pull between us picked up right where we had left off — with screaming and shoving and constant aggravation for us both. It all came to a head on my fifteenth birthday.

As always, I expected my mom to make a big fuss for my birthday. That was something she could be counted on to do — to make me feel special on my special day. But that year, just before my birthday, my mother announced we were all going to Texas for Hank's family reunion. She didn't know about the hell I had endured for years at Hank's mother's house, so she couldn't have known what a monumental betrayal this felt like to me. But even planning the trip on the weekend of my birthday was hurtful. I flat out told my mom I wasn't going. She and Hank and Jayson went without me, leaving me with my Aunt Bridget.

Staying with Aunt Bridget wasn't the problem. In fact, I loved being with her and her husband, Al. They were the ones who took us in after Hank fired his gun at me and we had nowhere else to stay. But as much as I loved Bridget and Al, it was my mom who'd always made my birthdays special. And now, as I was turning fifteen, she wasn't even around. My aunt and uncle brought me a chocolate cupcake with a single candle — a sweet gesture, but not enough to make up for what I felt I was missing.

Instead of getting something wonderful on my birthday, I lost something instead — I lost any belief that I mattered. I just gave up on the idea that I counted as a human being. If my mom didn't care enough about me to choose me over a violent ex-husband, then I certainly wasn't going to care about myself, either. The sense of self-hatred that had been seeping into my soul was taking over. I blamed myself for all the bad things that had happened, and I believed the reason people didn't put me first was because I didn't deserve to be first.

I began to believe I was worthless, and I decided if I wasn't worth anything, I was going to act that way.

Not long after I turned fifteen, I started high school, and that's when I began hanging out with boys. It was innocent at first. I'd meet a boy, and we'd drive around in his car and stay out as late as we could. I remember going to a party with an old childhood friend, catching the eye of a tall, cute teenager, and wanting so much for him to come up and talk to me. Thrillingly he did, and we got in his car and drove around and finally parked in an alley so we could talk. I had a curfew then — I think it was

11:00 p.m. — but I'd long since blown past that. Around three in the morning, a car screeched to a halt just in front of us outside the alley. It was his mother, and she wasn't exactly happy.

I don't remember if he got punished, but I know I didn't miss a beat. Not much later I took a fancy to the grandson of an elderly couple my mother knew from church. After the service, he and I got together, then drove around town and hung out all day and most of the night. This time it was a police cruiser that found us parked somewhere. An officer took me home, where my mother had my bags packed and waiting for me by the front door.

"You're going to Safe House," she told me. Safe House was a home for juvenile offenders.

After years of fights and hair-pulling brawls, my mother and I were hopelessly deadlocked. We spent 90 percent of our time waging battle against each other with no end to the hostilities in sight. It got to where I challenged her authority even when I knew she was right. I wasn't so much rebelling against her as rebelling against the world. The less control I felt over my life, the more I lashed out in anger and frustration. Finally my mom had had enough. She was ending the fight by shipping me away — and the truth is I was happy to go.

"Fine," I told her, "but don't ever come get me. I'm never coming back."

At Safe House, they told me I could stay for thirty days, and that sounded great: a whole month on my own without my mom around. The next morning, though, reality set in. A counselor woke me up at dawn and sent me to clean the communal bathroom. I was scrubbing filthy floors and toilets at 6:00 a.m. Another young girl who was there cleaning asked me what I was in for.

"I stayed out late," I answered. "What about you?"

"I stabbed my mom with scissors," she said.

That evening I called my mom and apologized and asked her to please, please come get me. And she did.

But if I was supposed to have learned some great lesson from my day at Safe House, I certainly did not. After that I became friends with an older girl from school, Jennifer, and she introduced me to real partying. She took me to the Air Force base, where some military guys were throwing a party, and I drank my first beer . . . and drank a few more . . . and got so drunk I finally passed out. Jennifer drove me home, but the next day I was so sick, I couldn't stop throwing up. I told my mother I had the stomach flu.

I wound up staying the night with Jennifer a lot, because she had no curfew and because she was always going to parties on the Air Force base. I liked hanging out with these cute young guys in their dorms. Before I knew it I was madly in love with one of them. He was darkly handsome with smooth tan skin and deep brown eyes. He was also incredibly sweet and attentive. On my birthday he gave me a bunch of beautiful long-stemmed roses, and I just about swooned. I was turning sixteen. He was twenty-two.

It was my first love affair, and I threw myself into it wholeheartedly. I was completely caught up in the sweeping passion of being in love. It felt like something that was all mine — something that no one could take away from me. Not long after that birthday, I willingly gave myself to a man for the first time.

Two weeks later, he dumped me. He said I was too young.

The euphoria of my first love was replaced by the utter despair of my first broken heart. Through all of the harm and hardship I'd endured in my childhood, I'd never felt anything so totally devastating. I lay in bed for hours and hours, listening to love songs and sobbing to my friends on the phone. My mother happened to be standing outside my bedroom during one of these calls, and that's how she found out we had slept together. When she came in to confront me, I expected her to really let me have it. So I was surprised when she sat on my bed and hugged me close. I guess I kept forgetting my mom was capable of great kindness.

It took me months to get over it, but slowly I got back in the rhythm of my regular high school life. Soon enough, a cute senior boy caught my eye. Phillip was one of the most popular guys in high school. He was tall and broodingly handsome, and he drove this awesome red truck. Everything about him was slick. We started hanging out and spending most nights cruising up and down Main Street in his nifty truck. That was what we did back then, when gas was around 82¢ a gallon — we'd drive down the street, turn around, and drive back, and do that all night long, honking at friends, jumping out and getting in different cars, stopping at Sonic for milk shakes, or pulling into parking lots just to horse around.

With Phillip, I tried marijuana for the first time. Then Phillip moved on to even harder stuff. Now, I wanted to be a bad girl, but I didn't want to be *that* bad. Sure, I drank too much now and then, but I had no interest in hard drugs. This caused problems for us, and Phillip and I started fighting pretty much every night. I was used to screaming matches as a way of life, so I didn't think this was all that unusual, or even unhealthy. But Phillip was beginning to treat me badly, blowing me off and calling me names and disappearing so he could hang out with his druggie friends.

Then, after one of our fights, Phillip picked me up and threw me through his screen door, and I tumbled down the front steps to the ground. He threw my purse at me and slammed the door, and I lay there crying and scooping up stuff that flew out of my purse. When my mom found out what Phillip had done, she took me to get a restraining order.

Another broken heart, another bout of wallowing. My self-esteem, which had always been bad, was hitting an all-time low. I dropped out of the high school dance team, because I believed I was too fat to wear the short-skirt uniform. In reality, I was a tiny thing, maybe five foot two and 110 pounds, but I was sure I was hideously fat and unattractive. The truth is, from the age of twelve and all through high school, I suffered from bulimia. It was another one of my dark secrets, and it was my way of exerting at least a little control over my life. One day my brother found out and ran to tell our mom. My secret was out, but it would be many more years before I finally put the demons behind that secret to rest.

Things spiraled downward from there. I dropped out of high school and got my mom to enroll me in an alternative school for students with social and disciplinary problems. Some of the students were kids who thought they were too cool for regular school and liked to party and drink and smoke pot, like me. Some of them had horrible home lives and just didn't fit in at regular schools. This school had no set hours; you just dropped in when you wanted to and studied what you liked. There were a lot of pregnant girls there and a lot of girls cradling their tiny brand-new babies. I think all of us were just searching for a better way and a brighter future. In a world where most of us had labeled ourselves failures, our new teachers were trying their best to make us realize we weren't.

Being at this school made me realize I wanted to be a teacher someday, too.

Around then I also got a job as a waitress

at the local Sizzlers, making something like $2 an hour plus tips. I wanted to save as much money as I could, to make myself more independent from my mom. I had my own car — a giant used tan Cutlass Supreme my mother got me for Christmas. I know I should have been grateful to her for getting me a car, but when I first saw it, I cried, and not out of joy. It was so big and so clunky and so *uncool;* I was absolutely mortified. During the winter it wouldn't even start, and I had to stick a ballpoint pen in some tube in the engine before turning the ignition. I think a drug cartel gangster must have owned it before me, because it had a gold-chain license plate and gold baubles all over the inside lining. It had no shocks and bounced like crazy over every little bump. I wound up going to school late and leaving early every day, so no one would see me pull up in my hideous car.

But that embarrassing car would come in handy soon enough. The fighting with my mother was getting worse, and we had another one of our epic battles. Somewhere in the middle of all the yelling and pushing and hair-pulling, my mom told me that if I didn't like her rules, I should leave. And that's just what I did.

I packed everything I owned into my enormous car and basically lived out of it for the next month. I stayed with friends and never missed school, and I savored my newfound freedom. For three weeks I didn't even bother to call my mom and let her know I was okay. Finally she showed up at school one day to tell me she loved me and was worried about me. Eventually I agreed to move back home, under one condition: no curfew. My mother was forced to concede that I was an adult now, and she promised to start treating me like one.

When I was seventeen, I met another man at a party. Dean had already been married and had custody of his three-year-old daughter. He was six years older than me, but I didn't care. I always felt older than my years, and I was used to hanging out with older people. Plus, I loved that Dean was so attentive and seemed to really like me. We went from zero to super-serious in a matter of days. He was the third great love of my crazy, teenage life.

But of course that love story, like the others, didn't last long. After a whirlwind summer it was over as suddenly as it had started. This time I didn't wallow as much, because I was excited about starting college. What I didn't know then, and what I would soon discover, was that my breakup with Dean wasn't as clean as I thought. In fact, it wasn't clean at all. One afternoon, my mother came home and found me crying uncontrollably on the living room sofa.

"What's wrong?" she asked. "Tell me what's wrong."

But I couldn't, because I was crying too hard. Finally, I gulped in enough air to blurt it out between sobs.

"Mom," I said, "I'm pregnant."

CHAPTER SEVEN

I'd been broken up with Dean for a month when I found out I was pregnant. Our breakup hadn't been especially dramatic; after three months of being together — going to the car races, me babysitting his young daughter — he told me he thought we should stop seeing each other. We were sitting on a wooden bench in a playground when he told me. I took off the class ring he had given me and threw it at him. And that was that. The breakup still hurt, but it just seemed to be the inevitable end to all my relationships.

When I told one of my girlfriends that I was late in my cycle, she took me to the drugstore to buy a pregnancy test. I took it to the bathroom of her parents' house, and when I was done, held up the strip to see the result, but I couldn't quite figure it out. My girlfriend took a look and suddenly her eyes got really wide. That very instant I knew I was pregnant.

I was seventeen years old and having a baby.

How did it happen? Well, I know *how* it happens. I mean, how could it happen to me? I was taking birth control pills that I got at our local health department, and I guess I may have forgotten to take a pill one day. Okay, maybe more than one day. It was a small act of carelessness, but it was enough to drastically change my life. No matter how grown up I convinced myself I was, I was really just a mixed-up child. And I sure wasn't ready for the responsibility of taking care of a child of my own.

The first thing I did after finding out was call Dean. He came over to my friend's house, and we sat on her bed and talked things through. He wasn't upset or angry or anything, but he was very clear about how he felt.

"I don't want any more children," he said. "If you get an abortion, I will pay for it. But if you have this baby, I won't be there for you."

It was the first time I'd heard the word "abortion" uttered in a conversation about me, and it hit me like a punch to the gut. I burst out crying, but Dean wasn't budging. He didn't blow up, and he wasn't mean —

he just said he didn't want anything to do with me or our child.

I went straight home and took another pregnancy test. The result was the same: a single pink plus sign. I lay down on the sofa and cried like I'd never cried before. The overwhelming sensation I felt was terror — an ice cold panic in my bones. *What happens now? What am I going to do? Did I just ruin my life?* Having a baby meant saying good-bye to all my grand plans and dreams. I wanted to go to an awesome college, and I wanted to be a teacher. Most of all, I wanted to get out of my hometown and see the world. But with this news, all those plans went out the window. I was seventeen, and I felt like my life was over.

That's when my mother came home for lunch and found me sobbing.

I'd been dreading telling her from the moment I found out. She blew her top when I missed my curfew; what was she going to do now that I was pregnant? I thought about lying to her, but when she walked in the living room, I felt the urge to just blurt it out. So I did. I told my mother I was pregnant.

Her face froze, and she stared at me and said, "How do you know?"

I told her I'd taken a test and the strip

was on my bed. She walked into my bedroom and didn't come out for forty-five minutes. I don't know what she did in there, but I was sure that when she finally came out, she'd give me a lashing like never before. I curled up tighter on the sofa, crying and bracing for the storm. After what seemed like forever, my mother came out of the bedroom, the test strip in her hand. I waited for the yelling, but it never came.

Instead, she came over, sat next to me, and pulled me in for a hug. I sobbed into her shoulder, amazed by her reaction.

"It's going to be okay," my mom said softly. "I don't care what anyone in this town says; you are going to hold your head high. I love you, and this is my grandkid. You will not be ashamed. *This does not define you.*"

I knew right then that I was having this baby.

My mother went with me for the ultrasound when I learned my baby's sex. The technician asked if I wanted to know, and I said I did. For whatever reason, I was hoping it was going to be a boy. My mom and I focused on the blurry ultrasound image, trying to make sense of what we were seeing.

"There," the technician said, pointing at

my little baby. "You're going to have a boy."

My mother says she fell in love with my son right then and there in the doctor's office. She tells him, "I've loved you since you were a kidney bean with legs."

By then I'd already been in love with my child for some time. I'd sit in my bedroom, hand on my big belly, feeling him kick, and I'd marvel at the depth and newness of the love I felt. I was still scared to death that my life was over, but at the same time I was thrilled by the idea of having someone all my own to love. My whole life I'd been desperate to love and be loved, and I had this deep wellspring of emotion and affection in my heart that, because of my difficult childhood and my terrible choice in men, just went untapped. But now I would have someone I could love without reservation, and someone who would love me back unconditionally.

Nevertheless, it was still a big deal to be seventeen and pregnant in our town. It is not something that sits well with most God-fearing people in the Bible Belt. My father and his family, for example, were devout Catholics, and I knew they'd be less than thrilled to find out I was having a baby. I kept the pregnancy a secret from my dad for several months, until he sent me an invitation to his wedding. He was marrying some girl who was just seven years older than me, and he wanted me to be in the wedding party. He kept telling me to send him my measurements so he could have my dress made, but I kept putting it off. Finally, just a month before the big day, I had no choice but to call him.

"I can't be at your wedding," I said.

"Why not?"

"Because I'm pregnant."

There was a long, excruciating silence on the other end, until after about a minute, my father finally spoke.

"I'm going to have to call you back," he said. Then he hung up.

I waited the rest of the day for his call, but it never came. It never came the next day, either. Or the next or the next. Two weeks passed before my father called me one afternoon. And when we spoke, he didn't mention the pregnancy — we just chatted about other insignificant things. I don't know why I felt so surprised and crushed by that. After all, I knew full well my father couldn't handle this kind of sticky situation. He preferred not to discuss it at all, and maybe even to pretend I wasn't pregnant.

My mother, on the other hand, did everything she could to make me feel good about my situation. She took me out shopping for baby clothes, dismissing the looks of disapproval my growing belly got. When I was seven months pregnant, she threw me a baby shower at her friend's home. There was a special cake, and I got diapers and a swing and a car seat. I felt really happy that day.

Most nights, however, I'd lie awake worrying about how I was going to raise this little boy on my own. I was already losing friends left and right, because I couldn't hang out and party like I used to. And once the baby came around, I was sure I wouldn't have any friends left at all. I would no longer fit into the only world I knew.

My mother had a wonderful friend, whom I called Aunt Connie, and I had asked her to be my Lamaze coach. I'm sure Aunt Connie could see how frightened I was, because one day she told me, "Crystal, you have options. If you feel you absolutely cannot handle this child, I will adopt him." I didn't say yes or no, but I kept her offer in mind all the way through the pregnancy. As I got nearer my due date, I honestly didn't have any idea what I was going to do. My life was hurtling forward like a roller coaster, and I was just holding on for dear life.

Then one Sunday I was sitting in church watching my mom sing in the choir when I felt a sharp pain in my lower back. I caught my mom's eye and motioned I was leaving, and I quickly drove back home. Aunt Connie came over, asked me some questions, and declared, "Crystal, you're in labor." I was only thirty-six weeks along, so I hadn't even packed a hospital bag yet. Aunt Connie packed one for me, and we drove to Comanche County Memorial Hospital, about thirty miles away in Lawton. I was admitted on Easter Sunday.

Aunt Connie told me the discomfort I was feeling was caused by contractions, and I remember thinking, *Wow, this pain isn't that bad.* Then they broke my water to speed up my labor, and the real contractions began. These were long, slow waves of pain that built and built and felt like they couldn't possibly get any worse, except they always did. The first one was so horrible and scary, I jumped out of bed and started putting my clothes on over my hospital gown. Aunt Connie looked at me in total confusion.

"Where are you going?" she asked.

"I can't do this," I said. "I'm leaving."

Aunt Connie burst out laughing. "Honey," she said, "it doesn't matter where you go; you're gonna have this baby."

They gave me an epidural so I could sleep a bit, and my mom showed up with a camcorder to tape the delivery. My doctor told me what was going to happen and how I had to push, and suddenly, I had only a single frightening thought: *Will I ever be able to give this child what he needs?*

Then everything happened at once. Nurses swarmed and the doctor got into position. My mother pressed record. I heard the doctor say push, so I pushed. I heard him say it again, so I pushed again. And then he didn't say anything, and I didn't know what was happening. I was terrified, until he stood up cradling something in his hands: this squirming little pink thing making funny noises.

In that moment, I met the love of my life. I met my son.

The doctor handed him to me, and I held him against my chest and looked at this tiny miracle in my arms. In a flash all my fears and worries and terrors went away. I loved my son deeply and instantly, and I knew that I always would. Aunt Connie never had to ask if I was keeping my child. Just from watching me with him in the first seconds of his life, she knew for certain that I was.

I named him Jameson Payne, the first part in honor of Grandma Ernie (that was her maiden name) and the second part because I just liked the name Payne. Inevitably, he became JP.

The euphoria of being a first-time mother is something I will never forget, but unfortunately that glow didn't last too long, either. Back at my mom's house the reality of my situation announced itself quickly and clearly, in the form of JP's wails through the night, every night. I'd imagined JP and I would sleep blissfully together, a mother and son cuddled up and lost in their own dream world. Instead, JP barely slept at all. He was born without a sucking reflex, so feeding him was nearly impossible. I had to tape a small tube to my finger, connect it to a syringe of milk, and hold the tube against the back of JP's throat, letting little droplets of sustenance trickle into his system. And I had to do that several times a night. It was a lot of work, and I wasn't sleeping at all. I was in over my head.

One night I sat next to JP's bassinet and watched him cry and cry, and I started crying right along with him out of sheer frustration. I picked him up and held him and rocked him, but nothing could stop his screaming. Finally I just gave up, and my son and I wept in unison in the long, dreary middle of the night.

And then, right on cue, my mother came into my bedroom. She'd been helping me with JP quite a bit in those early days, but still I tried to do everything myself because I didn't want to feel too dependent on her. I remember rolling up pennies and dimes so I could buy diapers without asking her for money. But when she came into my bedroom and asked, "Can I take him for a minute?" I was so relieved I nearly threw JP at her. I knew my mother had to get up early to go to work that morning, but I was so tired and so desperate for sleep that I let her walk JP around the living room while I lay down and closed my eyes. I woke up a couple of hours later, with JP sleeping peacefully in his bassinet.

My mother was my hero in those early days, and I will never forget all that she did for me.

It turns out my dad was actually pretty excited about having a grandson, too. He came down to see him not long after he was born, and when JP was about six months I took him up to Illinois to meet my dad's mother, Mardel (my grandfather had passed away when I was just a baby). Now, Mardel was an *extremely* private person. Even her own children didn't know very much about her. A few years before she died, Mardel wrote her own obituary, and when her sons read it, they didn't recognize any of the names from her side of the family. But they were also relieved they didn't have to write it, because none of them would have known what to say.

Not surprisingly, I was a little nervous bringing my baby to meet her. According to my dad, she didn't like her family's name to be a matter of any public discussion, good or bad, so her granddaughter having a baby out of wedlock couldn't have thrilled her. Still, I hoped for the best as my dad drove us over to her house in Illinois. When we got to the back porch, my dad said he had to tell me something.

"Um, your grandma doesn't know you have a child," he said, precisely two seconds before he rang the doorbell.

What? He'd never told her about JP? I didn't really have time to be shocked, because just then the door opened and Mardel was standing in front of me.

"Hi, Grandma," I said. "This is my son."

Mardel didn't say anything. She had a super-serious look on her face (but then I can't remember a time when she *didn't* have that look). She walked back into her house, opened a closet, and came back with a little stuffed clown. We sat in the living room,

123

and I watched with a smile on my face as Mardel played with JP and the clown. She wasn't overly affectionate — she never was — but neither did she say anything like, "How could you have done this?" or "Why didn't you tell me?" I remember feeling a huge sense of relief. Over the years Mardel was a really good great-grandmother to my kids, always sending them crisp five-dollar bills in their Christmas and birthday cards.

I wasn't the only one who felt relieved that day. My father later told me that as we stood on the back porch waiting for his mother, he was so nervous about her reaction, his knees were shaking. Looking back, that afternoon explains a lot about my father and our relationship. I didn't realize it then, but as we stood there on the porch, my father and I were both looking for the very same thing — approval. I didn't want him to be embarrassed by me and my child, and he didn't want his mother to be embarrassed by him and *his* child. And because of how private and distant his mother could be, my dad felt like he was always chasing after that approval — even as a grown man. Of course, that's just how it was for my dad and me. Because of how private and unemotional he was, I didn't always feel like I had his approval, either.

It had nothing to do with love — Mardel dearly loved her son, just like my dad loved me. It had to do with something that can be broken inside people, making it hard for true feelings to see the light of day.

When I look back at my teenage self, I feel so heartbroken for that lost young girl. I am saddened by everything she went through, and I wish deeply she had made better decisions along the way. But I know how much anger and bitterness she held in her heart, and I know how much she hated herself and considered herself worthless. I know how badly she wanted to believe in God and how hard it was for her to accept that He was listening. I wish I could hold her and tell her how special she is.

But of course I can't do those things. I can only tell you the truth of my life, no matter how painful it is.

Two years after JP was born, I had a summer fling with someone in town. It didn't mean anything, and it didn't last long. But then, one morning, I woke up feeling nauseous. I drove myself to see our family doctor. I described my symptoms, and the first thing she asked was, "Could you be pregnant?" I said no, absolutely not; I was using birth control. She gave me a few tests and came back thirty minutes later with the results.

"The tests were all negative," she said, "except for the pregnancy test. You are definitely pregnant."

I threw my head in my hands and wept. I can still recall the deep, deep shame I felt in front of that doctor. She tried to console me, but I just kept saying, "I can't do this again. I can't." I felt a sickening panic, a sense of utter doom. What was wrong with me? This time, I knew for sure I hadn't missed a single pill — not one! The doctor explained that pregnancies can sometimes still happen even when on the pill, and I thought, *Of* course *it would happen to me.* The doctor was so sweet to me, and she did her best to comfort me and make me feel like I had options.

"It's not the end of the world, Crystal, I swear," she said.

But I couldn't help feeling that it was.

There are many things I could have done at that point. I could have told my mother, who had been so kind and giving after my first pregnancy. I could have called Aunt Connie, who had been so ready to adopt my first child. I could have talked to a pastor or to a friend. I could have reached out for help, for guidance, for advice. I could have done any of those things.

But in the end I didn't call my mother. I didn't call Aunt Connie, either. I didn't talk to a pastor or to a friend.

All I did was pray to God for forgiveness.

Just three days after learning I was pregnant, I walked into a nondescript brick office building, went to the front desk, and handed over $300. They told me to have a seat in the waiting room, so I did.

Then I just sat in my chair and waited, too numb to feel anything at all.

CHAPTER EIGHT

I had found the clinic in the yellow pages, and I took the earliest appointment they had. Up until then, I'd never really given any serious thought to the issue of abortion. I knew that as a Christian I was supposed to be against it. I'd see bumper stickers that said, "It's a Child, Not a Choice," and deep down I knew it was wrong. Other times I'd try to convince myself that I should have the right to decide what to do with my own body. But suddenly this wasn't just a theological debate.

Suddenly it was real.

The clinic was in Oklahoma City, and I convinced a friend to come with me. We took the two-hour drive up Interstate 44 in my beat-up old Mustang GT, talking about everything except the most important thing. I felt myself shutting down a little more with each passing mile.

At the clinic I handed over my cash and

filled out some forms. Then I sat in the waiting room, listening for my name. I can't remember a lot about the clinic, except that it was drab and ordinary and might as well have been a dentist's office. And it was quiet, really quiet — no conversations, no laughter, just silence. I sat in my chair feeling like I was watching someone else go through this. There were a few other girls there, but I kept staring at the ground, afraid to make eye contact. I wondered what path had brought them to this place on the same day as me. I wondered if they had cried themselves to sleep the night before like I had, or if they'd begged God to forgive them and take care of their babies like I had. I wondered if their hearts were breaking as they sat there waiting to hear their names, like mine was.

Finally a nurse called for me and took me to another room. She handed me a few more papers and asked me to sign a waiver. I thought about how similar it all felt to a normal doctor's appointment, except there was nothing normal about it. The waiver, she explained, described how this was a serious medical procedure that could, like many other procedures, result in my death. I was shocked to hear the word "death," because I'd never thought for a moment that could happen. *How ironic is that?* I thought. *You come in here for an abortion, and you're the one who dies.* And then I had a second over-riding thought:

If you die, it'll be what you deserve.

Once I signed the papers, everything happened so quickly. I was taken to a procedure room where a nurse helped me change into a hospital gown. My legs were shaking, and I felt like I might throw up. "Do you want to be asleep or awake?" the nurse asked, and I didn't answer because I didn't know what I wanted. The numbness that had gotten me through the long drive was wearing off. Suddenly I was starting to panic.

"Do you want to see the fetus on the ultrasound?" another nurse asked as she laid me down on the table and put my feet in the stirrups.

"No, I don't want to see my baby," I said quickly. I surprised myself by using the word "baby." It was the first time I or anyone else had used it since I walked into the clinic. All at once, it struck me that what I was doing was unforgiveable. Around me, the nurses and technicians were casually going about their business, trying to keep the mood light. I couldn't understand how they could act so normally, as if I was about to get a molar removed, while to me it felt like something horrifying was happening. A doctor came in, and the pace of activity picked up even more.

Get up, Crystal, I thought. *Just get up, and tell them you changed your mind.*

But my body seemed frozen. And then the crippling panic began to subside as the anesthetic dragged me under. The next thing I knew, two nurses were helping me get dressed and hustling me into another room with several big recliners and fans blowing warm air around. A nurse handed me a cup of cold water.

"You'll feel light-headed for a while," she said.

For some reason, I didn't cry. I cried a lot in those days over every little thing, but there, in the clinic, not a single tear. I guess the only thing I felt at that moment was shock. *I can't believe you did this, Crystal,* I kept saying to myself. I sat in stunned silence, listening to the loud hum of the fans and the insistent voice in my head: *What have you done, Crystal? What have you done?*

The door swung open, and a nurse walked in with another girl. She was tall and skinny and quite beautiful, with long sandy brown hair and big, sad eyes. I guessed she was about seventeen or so. She could have sat in any one of the recliners spread around the room, but she picked the one next to me. She was crying uncontrollably, her chest heaving with every gasp for breath.

Then the girl looked over at me, and our eyes locked. We didn't say a word, because we didn't have to. We knew exactly what the other was feeling. It was this terrible mixture of shame and horror and disbelief, as if our souls had been torn from our bodies and then replaced, but all mangled and broken. But it was also this incredibly strong feeling of compassion for each other. In that moment, sitting in those cheap recliners with those big fans buzzing, we were giving each other some small measure of comfort at a time when we desperately needed it. We each served as a witness to what the other had endured. There was no judgment, just a shared pain that neither of us had the words to express. This wasn't just some routine medical procedure. We'd both lost something we could never get back. We'd made a choice we could never undo, as much as I would later pray that I could. When we walked out of that clinic, we'd be very different from the scared and anxious girls who had walked in. We'd both been changed profoundly and forever, and we knew it.

I don't know if that lovely girl ever thinks

of me, but all these years later I still think of her, and I hope and pray she has found forgiveness and happiness, wherever she is.

That night I begged God to forgive me for what I'd done. I asked Him over and over — *Please, God, forgive me for this, please.* I said these words night after night, week after week. *Please, please, please, God, forgive me.*

But even as I was saying them, I felt all but certain they would do no good. I couldn't see any possible way God could ever forgive me for what I'd done. Even if He was real, even if He was listening, there was no chance I would ever receive His forgiveness. I believed I was doomed, and I never felt more worthless as a human being. I was a sinner, a failure, unforgiveable, beyond salvation and hope. All those times I'd been baptized seemed almost silly to me now. I hadn't been saved or cleansed at all. The dirtiness of my world was something that could not be scrubbed away. I'd gone to church every Sunday as a child and a teenager, but in my twenties I stopped. Spiritually, I was finished.

I hated myself so much that whenever I passed a mirror I looked away, because I couldn't bear to see my own reflection.

I wasn't sure of much in my crazy life, but

I was sure of one thing: God could never, ever love me now.

I've been asked many times since I started sharing this part of my story where my heart lies in regard to abortion. This is what I say.

I say that my heart lies with the girl who just found out she is pregnant and is lying in bed and crying and scared and thinking about an abortion. I want to sit with her and tell her the truth about what she is contemplating. I want to tell her it is not the easy way out she may think it is; that in truth it will forever be her nightmare. That no matter how far or how fast she runs, she will never be able to outrun the conse-quences of that decision. That no matter how much time passes, she will always wonder about the child she never got the chance to meet.

My heart lies with the girl walking out of an abortion clinic. I want to take her and hold her and wipe away her tears. I want to tell her she can never fall so far that God won't catch her and love her and above all else forgive her. I want to tell her that God never stopped loving her and that His arms are still open to her if only she will choose Him. I want to tell her that with God there is always hope and always love and always forgiveness. But I also know that forgiving herself will be her biggest battle.

My heart lies with the women who have been covered by a curtain of shame, women who keep their abortions a secret and can't grieve for the child they lost because of the crippling guilt that holds them captive. I want to sit them down and tell them about the God I met. The God who is the key that will unlock their chains, if only they will raise their chains to Him.

And finally, my heart lies with the millions of babies who have not been granted a chance at life. I cry for these little lives that have no voice. I see the statistics that say more than 50 million babies have been aborted since it became legal in the United States, and I can't help but cry and grieve for the one baby that was mine. The lie of the enemy is a powerful thing, and I know all too well the destruction that it causes.

After the abortion, I acted as normally as I could around people, so no one would think anything was wrong. At nights I put myself through the ringer, praying and crying. But during the days, everything, at least outwardly, looked fine. And then after a few months I slipped back into my normal routines and went on with my life. My wounds turned into scars.

It wasn't too long before I fell in love again. Will was someone I knew from way back in the sixth grade, when I was a tomboy trying to hold my own with the tough boys in my class. The boys wouldn't let you play with them during recess if they thought you were a sissy girl, so no matter how much they pulled my hair or knocked me down, I always got up and jumped right back in with them. After a while, they let me be part of their little playground gang.

Will was one of those tough little boys. I saw him again years later when he was all grown, and I thought, *Gosh, he's really cute.* He had long black hair like a rock star, and he always wore the most amazing leather jacket. I learned he had a reputation as someone you didn't want to mess with. He wasn't all that big or muscled, just quick on his feet and street-smart. He was also a talented artist who did these incredible air-brushed drawings. He could be very sweet to me, and he was wonderful with JP. I began to see a real future for us.

But, like all my other loves, Will was volatile and unreliable. He liked to drink and have a good time with his pals. We broke up constantly, only to get back to-gether again. That should have been all the warning I needed, but I was too young and too in love to see all the giant red flags unfurling before my eyes.

Roughly at the same time, Will and I decided to get married *and* I got pregnant again. This time, though, it was no accident or surprise. You see, in my talks with God I'd been begging Him to send the baby I'd lost in my abortion back to me. I longed for that child — I *grieved* for that child — and I begged God for another chance. I wanted the emptiness inside me to be filled. And in my brokenness I guess I believed I could make everything right by replacing the child I had aborted. And so when I learned I was pregnant again, I was ecstatic. I believed I'd been given a second chance.

My mom wanted to plan a big, splashy wedding, but when I told her I was pregnant, we agreed on a smaller ceremony. She wasn't thrilled to hear I was having another baby, but by then I didn't much care what anyone thought of me. I asked my father to walk me down the aisle, and I was delighted when he said yes. The service was at a tiny little Methodist church in town, and we invited something like thirty friends and relatives. Right before the ceremony, as I was standing in the back of the church with my father, he noticed I was crying.

"You don't have to go through with this," he told me. "We can get in my car right now and drive away."

"I'm not crying about that," I said. "I'm crying because my pantyhose are too tight and it took me thirty minutes to get them on and I have to go to the bathroom!"

The ceremony was short and sweet. I wore a simple white dress with red roses in my hair. Will looked so handsome in his dark suit and tie, and my beautiful son, JP, who was two, was just adorable in his little white button-down shirt. After the wedding we had a small reception in the church with cake and drinks and dancing. That was the day I truly realized I wasn't a kid anymore. I was a wife, with a son and a husband and a family of my own. It was one of the happiest days of my life.

I wish I could say the rest of the marriage was as warm and wonderful as the wedding, but I can't. Even before I married Will, there were clear signs we shouldn't be together. But once again, I ignored them. Maybe I was so used to seeing anger and discord in relationships that I figured that's how all relationships are. Or maybe I was so desperate to finally find some happiness, I simply pretended the warning signs weren't there.

The problem was that Will liked to

drink . . . a lot. Early on, he spent more time drinking with his friends than he spent with me, but I figured that since we loved each other, we'd have plenty of time later to grow and mature as a couple. I truly believed we would spend the rest of our lives together. I didn't realize we were already tearing apart.

We lived together in a small house we rented in town, about seven miles from where I grew up. Some nights Will would come home late from drinking and pass out. Other nights I'd wake up in the darkness and look for him, only to find him gone. I'd get ready to go searching for him, but inevitably my car would be gone, too. Or he'd tell me he was going to the store and would see me in five minutes, then disappear for hours. When he was around, we fought constantly — loud, nasty fights like the ones I'd known all my life.

A couple of weeks before Thanksgiving, the electricity in our house went out. I thought, *That's weird. I just gave Will money to pay the bill.* Two days later, the gas went out, too. Then I discovered we were two months behind on the rent. I had no choice but to move back in with my mom. I was eight months pregnant at the time.

My mother was the first to notice what I

was too willfully blind to see. She could see that Will's behavior was getting worse: more disappearances, more fights, more unexplained events. Finally one day she sat me down and told me the score.

"Your husband is doing drugs."

I didn't want to believe her. I told her no, that's impossible, but my mother knew the signs all too well. Before long, I realized she was right: Will was hopelessly hooked on drugs. And not the measly stuff I dabbled in — hard-core drugs.

That realization ripped my heart apart. I was devastated, but not only for myself — though it was agonizing to see my dream of wedded bliss get so quickly and cruelly squashed. My heart also broke for Will, because I knew that, like me, he never really got a fair chance at having a normal life.

Will's childhood was even darker than mine. He was one of eight kids who grew up in extreme poverty, in a rat-and-roach–infested house that was unfit to live in. His family barely had money for food, let alone clothes. I later learned the reason William wore his leather jacket all the time was because he didn't want anyone to know he had only two shirts.

Will's brothers and sisters had many different fathers, and the man listed on Will's birth certificate wasn't even his real dad. Maybe because he didn't belong to the man who was called his father, Will didn't feel like he belonged to anyone at all. Will told me that he met his real dad only a handful of times, and that when he was eight years old, he watched his father stab someone nearly to death. Years later he would learn his father had been killed.

A year before our wedding his older sister was murdered. Her body washed ashore on a riverbank. It fell to Will to go to the morgue and identify her body. He was in that morgue for only a few seconds, but I'm sure those few seconds damaged him down to his soul. And I am sure that when he closes his eyes, he can still see his sister's body.

Both Will and I were running away from our damaged lives, but instead of running to each other, we ran in different directions. He ran to drugs; I ran to motherhood. All the pain and shame and anger we both felt aren't things you can ever outrun. Will and I were doomed from the beginning.

Three weeks before my due date, Will showed up at my mom's house and finally admitted he had a problem. We got him to agree to enter rehab after our child was born. It might seem like the birth couldn't have come during a crazier time, but to me it didn't feel that way at all. To me, it felt like my child was born in a moment of pure goodness and love.

And when my daughter arrived, I couldn't wait for the doctor to hand her to me. I stared at her little face with tears running down my cheeks. She had the sweetest little mouth and the most beautiful brown eyes I'd ever seen. I named her Sabyre, and she was my angel sent from heaven to heal my broken soul.

I now had two beautiful, healthy children . . . and one crumbling marriage. Will checked into rehab as promised, but while he was gone I realized I was ready to start a new life for my kids. And I was ready to do it on my own. I didn't want them to grow up with parents who fought constantly. I wanted something better for them and for me, plain and simple.

Simple, maybe, but definitely not easy. During our divorce proceedings Will took my car, so I had to ask friends to drive me back and forth to the diner where I worked the midnight shift. I'd earned my associate's degree a few weeks before Sabyre was born, and I was desperately trying to save enough money to go back and earn my bachelor's degree. More than anything I wanted to show my kids that, no matter how deep the hole you fall into, you can always claw your way out. But, boy, was the hole I found myself in deep.

One night a friend drove me and my kids home after my shift. It was around 4:00 a.m. when I opened the front door to find there was no heat or electricity. I immediately knew Will was responsible. Because he and I were still legally married, he was able to shut off my utilities and take my deposit money. By then I understood that addiction can be stronger than any love he might have felt. Love for me, love for his child, love for himself.

Standing in the darkness, I felt the cold winter wind blasting right through the apartment. It was one of those moments that makes you take stock of your life, and I stood there doing just that. I had no heat, no electricity, no money, and no phone — and my children were freezing.

"Are you serious, God?!" I screamed into the darkness. "How much more can I take?"

I bundled up JP and Sabyre, put them in their double stroller, and started walking to my mother's house seven miles away. It was the longest, coldest walk of my life. The streets were dark and empty; all the other families were safe and warm in their homes. And here we were, out in the street, trudging slowly into the frigid wind. I walked on, block after deserted block, constantly tucking my children beneath a blanket to shield them from the icy gusts. But I was feeling the cold in my bones, and I knew they must be, too. And with miles still to go I began to worry that we were in real trouble.

Just then, I saw the headlights of a car heading toward me. The car drove up alongside us and stopped. It was a taxicab. "Can I give you a ride to where you're going?" the elderly cabbie asked.

"I don't have any money," I said.

He got out of the cab and came up to me. "Don't worry about that," he said. "Let's just get those little babies in the car."

The cabbie drove me to my mother's house and helped me to the front door. I thanked him over and over and told him I'd find a way to pay him back, but he just shook his head and smiled.

"Someday you will do something good for someone else," he said.

I never learned his name or saw him again, but I also never forgot what he did and what he said. I often wonder now if God sent that man to save us. Whether He did or not, we were rescued that night.

■ ■ ■ ■

Will and I were divorced six months after the wedding. My kids were all that mattered to me after that, and I was determined not to bring any more bad influences into their lives. I went back to college to finish my degree, and I got a good-paying job as a waitress at the local country-western bar. Things were definitely looking up for my little family. But I was also very young and very lonely. Still, I figured that after Will, the consequences of my choices in men could hardly get any worse.

Tragically, in 2002, they did.

For a while I dated a man named Steven. We didn't stay together for long, but our breakup was friendly. Steven would drop by my house every once in a while to pick up something he'd left there. One winter afternoon, he pulled up in the driveway on a gleaming black motorcycle. JP, who was six years old, took one look at it and said, "Cool! Can I go for a ride?"

"Absolutely not," I said. Steven gunned the engine, and JP, standing mesmerized on the front porch, begged me to let him ride. But I held firm; I didn't want my son on the back of anyone's motorcycle.

Just then Sabyre, who was three and a half, had to go to the bathroom. I ran her inside, and when I came back, both Steven and JP were gone. Now, I knew Steven was a gentle man and would never intentionally harm JP, but that didn't make me any less furious. I stood on the porch boiling and thinking, *How dare he take my son?* I also felt a hard, sickening feeling in my stomach, like someone had hit me with a bat.

Then I heard the sirens.

I threw Sabyre in her car seat and jumped behind the wheel, following the wailing sirens. Four blocks from my house, I saw a police car parked sideways closing off a street and about a dozen people standing around. I ran up to a bystander and frantically asked what happened.

"There's a wreck," he said. "Some guy crashed."

"Was there a motorcycle?" I screamed.

The man looked at me, and I saw fear flash in his eyes. Softly he said, "Yes."

The next two things I saw are things that haunt me still.

I saw a fireman sitting on a curb with his head in his hands, weeping.

And I saw JP's little black tennis shoes — with Velcro straps because he couldn't tie laces yet — lying on their sides in the middle of the street.

Where is God in a moment like this? some may ask. Where was God on that blocked-off street with the weeping fireman and the shoes ripped off my son's feet? Why does Hebrews 13:5–6 tell us that God promised, "Never will I leave you, never will I forsake you"? What comfort can that be on a day as horrifying as that particular one in 2002?

Back then, I wasn't aware of the reality of God's presence here on Earth. I hadn't yet learned that our worst times must also be the times when our faith in God is strongest. I didn't know that God is with us in our suffering, and that suffering can bring us even closer to Him. As hard as it can be for us to believe, our very worst moments are precisely when God's grace is most brightly revealed. "We also glory in our sufferings," it says in Romans 5:3–4, "because we know that suffering produces perseverance; perseverance, character; and character, hope." God is with us always. God never leaves us. God will never forsake us. I know these things now, but I would only learn them after I died and saw what I saw, there in heaven, alongside my angels.

I was aware of my guardian angels on my left, and I instantly knew them and loved them and realized they'd always been by my side. But I was also aware of a being on my right, and instantly I knew who this was, too. And what overcame me was a profound, endless desire to praise and worship this being, for I knew immediately I was in the presence of God.

I have always referred to God as a him, and I guess I always will. But the being on my right was not a him or a her; it was just God. Nor did I make any distinction between God, Jesus, and the Holy Spirit, as we sometimes do on Earth. They were all One — the One before me now. There was no distinct form, certainly no face or body, just a blinding profusion of brightness. I wasn't so much meeting God as I was *recognizing* Him. I already *knew* Him, and He knew me. I'd spent my life doubting His existence and disbelieving His love for me, but in that instant I knew God had always, always been there — right there with me.

And while I say God was on my right and I had the sensation of turning to my right toward Him, what I really experienced was the understanding that *everything* around me was of God. The light, the brightness, the angels, the communication — everything was a creation of God. I understood that I was a part of Him, and that's the moment I truly realized what being a creation of God truly means.

There was another sensation — a sensation that I wasn't just aware of God; I was *feeling* Him. His radiance wasn't simply something I could observe; it was something that overwhelmed every sense I had. In heaven we don't have just five senses; we have a *ton* of senses. Imagine a sense that allowed us to not only see light, but also to taste it. Imagine another sense that allowed us to touch and feel light. Imagine yet another sense that isn't taste or touch but some *new* way to experience something, creating a more amazing and rewarding connection than any of our earthly senses allow.

That is what I experienced in the presence of God — a beautiful new way of receiving and sending love. I was completely *infused* by God's brightness and His love, and I wanted to enter *into* His brightness and intertwine myself completely with it. I felt a miraculous closeness to God but wanted to feel even *closer.*

This was the Creator of the universe, and I was in His presence! The sheer ecstasy of it! The beauty of it, the joy and the grace, the way my spirit soared and my heart burst — how I wish I had the words to convey just how miraculous this was. It was the blessing of all blessings, and I knew that I was changed forever.

In the very same instant that I saw and knew and recognized God, I immediately confessed that He was my Lord and worshipped Him with all my might. The Bible has a passage that says, "every tongue will confess and every knee shall bow," and let me tell you, that's what this was like. A complete surrender to His greatness and an overpowering desire to praise and worship Him. On Earth, there were times during worship in church when my feet hurt or my kids were fussing, and I'd think, *Are we almost done?* But this was different, *very* different. With every fiber of my existence I wanted to praise and worship God, and that's *all* I wanted to do. And I wanted to do it *forever.* And I *felt* like I could do it forever. And so that's what I did, happily, joyously — I praised God.

What drove my praise was the intensity and immensity of my love for God. There is simply no other love remotely like it. When I was in His presence, I just had the feeling that I loved Him so, so much — more than I ever thought was possible. "You shall love the Lord your God with all your heart, and with all your soul, and with all your mind, and with all your strength," Jesus said when asked which commandment was the most important, and that is how I felt — like I loved God with absolutely everything — *everything* — I had.

And you know, back on Earth, I had so many questions for God. "If I ever meet Him," I'd say, "I'm going to ask Him how He could let someone molest me when I was a child. How could He abide brutality against children or the suffering of starving people or cruelty toward the weak? How could He allow such evil to exist in the world?"

Why, I would ask Him, was he such a punishing God?

But in heaven, all those questions immediately evaporated. In His presence I absolutely understood that in every way God's plan is perfect. Sheer, utter perfection. Does that mean I can now explain how a child being murdered fits into God's plan? No. I understood it in heaven, but we aren't meant to have that kind of understanding here on Earth. All I can tell you is that I know God's plan is perfect. In His radiance, it all makes perfect, perfect sense.

In this way all the questions I had for God were answered without me even having to ask them. And yet, standing in His glorious presence, filled with His infinite wisdom, there was still one question I felt compelled to ask. No sooner had I found myself in heaven than I became thunderstruck by the most glaringly obvious failure of my life on Earth, and that is what compelled me to ask this question of God.

But in fact it wasn't really a question for God at all.

It was a question for myself.

CHAPTER NINE

When my mother was young, her parents changed hometowns like some people change shoes. By the time she was fifteen, she'd moved at least a dozen times. When she grew up and had her own kids, she repeated the pattern, packing us up and finding new places to live whenever things got too sticky. Then it was my turn. In the eight years after I had my children, we lived in twelve different homes in three different cities. Some people are stayers, planting deep roots. Some people are runners, always escaping something. I was a runner. When things went bad, I ran. But you can only run so far and so fast before you finally catch up with yourself.

Much of the time I was running away from men. I was fleeing nightmares dressed up as fairy tales. But if I am being truly honest about why I wound up in so many failed relationships, I can't just blame the men.

My relationships fell apart for different reasons, sometimes by my choice and sometimes not, but there was one thing that stayed the same, one obvious constant: *me.* I was someone who could not be alone, who feared darkness and solitude — a creature who turned to men to escape her demons.

And of course I was missing the one relationship that could have spared me all of this torment. I had not yet realized the most important partner anyone can have is God.

Don't get me wrong — I'm not saying there was a huge conga line of men in my past. There really wasn't. I liked *being* in relationships, so I usually stayed in them for a long time — usually too long. The sad truth is, I was introduced to men when I was just three years old, and that affected all the relationships that followed. I'm not going to tell you about all of them, because there's no point in doing that, really. I just want you to know how I got from where I was to where I ended up — at the scene of a crash on a winter's day, looking for my son.

After my divorce from Will, I got my job in the country-western bar. It was just like any other honky-tonk, a place where couples did two-steps and line dances and downed a lot of cheap beer. It was there I met a man named Nick. He was a little older than me and rugged and charming — and he was also about to ship out for three months of training. When he asked me for my number, I saw no harm in giving it to him, since I figured he wouldn't be around.

While he was away we spent hours talking on the phone and sending each other long e-mails. And when he came back, he was kind and attentive and constantly saying how beautiful I was. One night he told me he loved me and that he'd never felt this kind of love for anyone before. By then I was in love, too, in the only way I knew how to be — head over heels.

So when I learned the truth about Nick — that he was married, with two small children — it was too late. He swore to me that his marriage was over, that he'd soon be divorced, that he wanted to spend the rest of his life with me, and I allowed myself to believe him. I'd learn soon enough that Nick told *many* other women he loved them like no one else. My poor heart was starting to feel like a piñata.

Even worse, I was now an adulterer.

Something clicked for me after that. I vowed I would never, ever let another man break my heart. After Nick, I let go of that reckless, blinding yearning for passion and romance and gigantic love. I built a wall around myself, and for years I never let anyone in.

Unfortunately I didn't stop dating altogether. For a while I moved to Charleston to be with one man, then moved to Delaware when that didn't pan out too well. There were a couple of airmen — flyboys, we called them — who were appealing to me, because they were set to deploy and thus would be out of my life before they could do any damage.

One of them, it hurts me to say, was also married, something that should have stopped me but didn't. It wasn't that I was an uncaring person; it's that emotionally I had all but bottomed out. I didn't stop and think about how my actions were causing someone else pain. And anyway, I told myself, it wasn't me cheating. That was his problem, not mine. The truth is, my relationship with him was easy for me: no feelings, no commitment, and no broken heart. Today, it kills me to think of the wives and the children of cheating men. I'm sure I've contributed in some way to a family falling apart, and that fills me with immeasurable sadness. I should have had so much more respect for other people — and so much more respect for myself.

But back then, I was juggling my life the best way I knew how. I went to school all day, spent a few hours with my babies before putting them to sleep at my mom's house, then went to the bar and slung beers all night. I was exhausted, but, for the most part, I was happy. I had friends, I was saving money, and I was working toward my goal. My dream of finishing school and creating a better life for my kids was in sight. We were finally going to have the normal and wonderful life I'd always wanted, and no man was going to get in the way of that.

Then came Steven and the day he pulled up on his motorcycle.

What if Sabyre hadn't needed to go to the bathroom that very moment? What if I'd pulled JP inside along with us? What if I hadn't dated Steven in the first place? What if the world had spun slightly differently that day?

When I came out and saw JP was gone, I also noticed Steven's helmet sitting on the driveway. He hadn't even bothered to put his helmet back on, and I knew JP didn't have one, either. I stormed back inside seething with anger, waited a few minutes, then got in my car and drove to my mom's house nearby. I figured Steven might have taken JP there, but he hadn't. I drove back home and tried to busy myself with work, but when I looked at the clock, I noticed JP had been gone half an hour. All at once, I felt that sickening heaviness in my stomach, and an urgent thought popped in my head: *Get your shoes on.*

Just seconds later, I heard the sirens.

The police had blocked off Libra Street, and I remember thinking, *Oh, that's my sign.* Libra is the one with the scales of justice — the goddess of balance. Ironic, since my life was all about extremes. I pushed through the ring of spectators and saw the fireman sitting on the curb, his body slumped, his head in his hands. Then I saw those tiny black sneakers, the ones with the Velcro straps. JP was in kindergarten and hadn't quite learned to tie his shoelaces yet, so I got him shoes with straps. I don't know why he was having so much trouble learning how to tie laces; he just was. And now those sneakers were in the street, the Velcro straps still fastened.

I started running toward the sneakers, and two cops came forward and stopped me. "That's my son!" I screamed at them. "Where is he? Is he okay?" One officer put his hand on my shoulder and tried to calm me down; the other one knelt and zipped up Sabyre's winter coat.

"An ambulance just took your son away," the officer said.

He didn't say whether JP was alive or dead, or seriously injured, or anything — just that he wasn't there. Behind him I saw a delivery truck and a motorcycle on its side. I had another thought, clear as day: *This is it. This is your punishment.*

It took me many months to find out exactly what happened, and only then because I met someone who lived on Libra Street and saw the crash.

Steven and JP were cruising on the motorcycle; no one can be sure how fast. My little boy was sitting in front of Steven, not behind him. Up ahead at the intersection, a pizza delivery truck was approaching from the right. There was a yield sign there, and the truck's driver should have yielded but didn't. He was only a teenager himself. The truck blew past the yield sign, and Steven saw it coming into his path. According to police, Steven tried to swerve to the right, but it was too late. He hit the delivery truck head-on.

The first people on the scene saw Steven sprawled on the street, bleeding and unconscious. But there was no sign of JP at all. For a long time, they believed Steven was the only victim.

Then one of the responders crouched down to tend to Steven and happened to glance under the pizza truck. What he saw made him gasp and stagger to his feet.

"Oh, my God, there's a child under there!" he yelled.

JP had been thrown under the truck. He was thrown at such a speed that his little head wedged inside the front fender well, and he dangled there, his legs and arms limp like a rag doll. The firemen arrived, and one of them crawled beneath the truck and sawed through the fender well to free him. That was the fireman I saw on the curb. The sight of my son's skinny little body pinned and twisted inside the metal was just too much for him. He sat and cried for a boy he knew was somebody's heart and soul.

Once I learned JP wasn't there anymore, I grabbed Sabyre and drove like crazy to my mom's house to pick her up. Then I sped the half mile to the hospital, blasting the horn. My mother pounded the dashboard in agony. I burst through the doors of the ER and searched frantically for JP. A nurse corralled me and asked me to fill out paperwork, but I just kept screaming and banging on a door, trying to get to my son.

"He's just a baby!" I found myself yelling. "He's just a baby."

A nurse finally took me to the room where they had JP. I saw my son lying in a bed, crying, and I realized he was alive. His face was badly scratched and swollen, so swollen I could hardly recognize him. His tiny, delicate lips were mangled and streaked with blood. His right arm was broken and in a sling, and his left knee was sliced open and battered. Bits of asphalt and gravel were stuck on his face and in his hair.

I went to JP and put my hand gently on him and said, "I love you. I'm so sorry." I said this at least twenty times while I picked the gravel out of his hair. He was in too much pain to say or do much besides whimper; he just lay there, busted and broken, slipping in and out of consciousness. It was one of the most helpless feelings I've ever had in my life.

At some point, a doctor came over and told me JP was, in his words, "fine." I took that to mean he was going to survive, because he sure as heck wasn't fine. Then the doctor explained Steven's injuries were more severe, and he might not make it. I hadn't paid much attention to Steven, who

161

was in his own bed a few feet away. He needed brain surgery, and they were going to rush him to another hospital for an emergency operation. I wanted to be mad at Steven — I wanted to scream in his face, "How could you?!" — but I couldn't be angry until I knew he would survive.

And then, once I knew he'd live, I could say, "I'm gonna kill you."

Steven underwent emergency brain surgery and pulled through. In the end he sustained some brain damage but recovered more or less fully. The doctors told me JP had suffered a closed-head injury, meaning he got knocked around pretty good but there was no gash or opening. The worst, it seemed, hadn't happened. JP was a mess and in a great deal of pain, but he was alive. He would live, and he would be okay.

On that day and in the days that followed, I talked a lot to God. You might think I cursed Him, but I didn't. I knew in my heart the crash had been my fault. I'd made so many bad decisions in my life, and now one of those bad decisions had nearly killed my son. This was not God's fault. I believed deep down this was a consequence of the life I was leading. I'd committed many sins, and now it was time for the price to be paid.

And so I didn't curse God like I did when

my grandmother died. I hoped, though He couldn't possibly love me, that He would still love my innocent children. So I began praying again, this time begging God to heal my son.

A couple of days after the crash, I called JP's father to let him know what had happened. I'd had very little contact with him, besides constantly fighting to get him to include JP on his insurance, which he was legally bound to do but kept putting off. Still, I felt JP should speak with his father, and I got them together on the phone. I stood beside JP's bed and could hear his father's voice through the receiver, but all JP kept saying was "Hello? Hello?" Then JP dropped the phone and looked at me and said, "No one is there."

My heart sank like a brick. He couldn't hear out of his right ear. My boy wasn't "fine" after all. The punishment was just beginning.

CHAPTER TEN

The doctors confirmed JP had lost all hearing in his right ear. It turned out his whole face was paralyzed on the right side, but no one realized that until the swelling went down. He couldn't close his right eyelid, so they gave him a black eye patch, which he thought was pretty cool. The right side of his mouth just drooped, like half a frown. But the worst thing was how much pain he was in from his broken arm and mangled leg. Every movement caused him to seize up and moan. A physical therapist came by every day, but JP *hated* his therapy. He'd be alert when it was just me in the room, but as soon as he saw the therapist in the hall, he'd pretend to be fast asleep.

My sweet little boy, my fidgety little rascal of a son, could now barely move without terrible pain. I had to pick him up just to get him to the bathroom. "Mama, carry me," he'd say in a soft murmur. It filled me with shame and sadness to see him this way.

As soon as I realized JP was in for a long recovery, I dropped out of my college classes so I could be with him. He spent ten days in the hospital, and in that time the doctors never gave us a good diagnosis of what was wrong with him. They wanted to wait six months and run more tests before they reached a conclusion. I brought JP home, and over time his swelling went down and his paralysis went away. But he still couldn't hear out of his right ear, and walking was still a major challenge.

Because of his injuries, I had to keep JP out of kindergarten for several weeks. But not long after he got out of the hospital I took him back to his classroom so he could grab his books and say hi to his friends. I was getting ready to carry him down the long hallway to his classroom, but JP wouldn't let me near him — he didn't want anyone to see me carrying him. Instead, he limped his way down the hall all on his own. Had I carried him, it would have been a thirty-second walk; it took JP thirty-five agonizing minutes. It was all I could do not to sweep him up and cradle him in my arms.

Finally we got to his room, and JP proudly showed off his cast to his little buddies. Once we were back in the hallway and the door to his classroom was safely closed, JP looked at me with his sad eyes and said, "Mama, will you carry me?" I picked him up and kissed him gently and carried him to the car.

Most of the time, JP couldn't do much more than sit around the house with his leg propped up. Even taking baths was a nightmare, since he couldn't get his right arm or his left leg wet. It was like playing a cruel game of Twister in two feet of water. But, you know, we actually laughed a lot during bath time. Keeping different sides of his body out of the tub was so ridiculously hard, we *had* to laugh. And I know JP got a kick out of how I usually ended up more sopping wet than he was. Seeing him laugh at his own predicament was, for me, a great sign. That's when I realized he'd inherited my ability to laugh during even the hardest times. I'd passed something on to my son that was good and useful. It made me feel like JP was going to be okay.

However, something even scarier was going on. In the months after the accident, JP's behavior started to change. He'd go from extremely happy one minute to angry and irritated the next. He'd wake up in a great mood, then suddenly start acting as if his dog had died. He'd always been a little hyper — when he was five, he was diagnosed with attention deficit disorder — but these new outbursts were something completely different. He'd throw horrible tantrums, hurling himself to the floor kicking and screaming. He would lash out and punch and kick at me, too.

He'd also get strangely fixated on things. Sometimes he'd tell me the same thing over and over — forty or fifty times. I'd say, "Yes, honey, I know," and he'd say, "No, you're not listening!" and tell me again. Or he'd remember seeing a particular sign at Walmart and talk about it nonstop and demand to see it again. He'd be so upset, I'd have to get up in the middle of the night and drive him to Walmart so he could see the sign and come back home and finally fall asleep.

For two years after the accident we bounced from doctor to doctor, searching for something that would make JP better. That was a really frustrating time. One doctor insisted the tantrums were caused by JP's attention deficit disorder. I said, "No, this is not that. This is totally different."

The doctor replied, "Well, how would *you* act if you got hit by a truck?"

It was like I was fighting the whole world. JP was supposed to be listed on his father's insurance, but of course he wasn't yet. Even though his dad knew how important it was for JP to have good insurance, he kept putting it off, month after month. As a result, I had only state-sponsored insurance, which wouldn't pay for JP to see the specialists he needed. It took two whole years before we finally got in to see a doctor who gave me a good explanation of what had happened to my son.

The ear, nose, and throat specialist explained that the impact of the crash had jarred JP's brain stem. At the base of that stem are bundles of nerves that control different functions. One of them controls facial movements, while another controls the ability to hear. The crash had damaged those two nerves, which explained JP's paralysis and his loss of hearing. One of them had healed, and JP got his facial movements back. But the other wasn't healing, which is why JP still couldn't hear out of one ear.

There was nothing wrong with my son's ear; there was something wrong with his brain. Now I was on a mission to find someone who could fix it.

In the end, JP's diagnosis was much more serious than a closed-head injury. He had what they call a traumatic brain injury, which can mean all kinds of brain damage. I read everything I could about traumatic brain injuries, including a book by a woman who was an expert in the field and charged $20,000 to evaluate a patient. Well, I barely had $20 to give her, but I called her anyway and told her about JP. She was kind enough to let me read his medical records to her over the phone and to tell me what questions I should be asking his doctors. She helped me understand what was happening and what kind of tests JP needed. She was an angel who came out of nowhere and made me feel like I wasn't fighting this fight by myself after all.

Through all that research I learned that JP really needed to see a neuropsychologist, but my insurance wouldn't pay for that kind of specialist. A neuropsychologist became my personal Wizard of Oz — someone I had to find at any cost, no matter the hardship, in order to save my son. But try as I might, I was never able to get JP in to see one. All I could do was manage JP's outbursts and fixations as best I could and keep searching for the elusive Wizard.

Finally things came to a head.

One day when I picked up JP from the day care where he stayed after school, one of his teachers came over to talk. From the anguished look on her face I could tell it wasn't going to be idle chit-chat. She said she'd tried her best to be patient, but she just couldn't watch JP anymore. His outbursts were getting worse: he was throwing himself to the ground and punching himself, hard. His mood swings were getting more and more extreme. She was exhausted from trying to help him, and she was afraid he was going to really hurt himself. I begged her to give me a couple more weeks while I figured out what to do. Reluctantly she agreed.

By then, however, I was pretty much at the end of my rope, too. It was killing me to see JP struggle with himself so much and to see how he couldn't understand what was happening inside him. We both felt so powerless and frustrated and angry. And, like his teacher, I was worried JP was going to harm himself. He was getting bigger and stronger, and his outbursts were getting more violent. Every day was another opportunity for something tragic to happen.

Finally someone told me about a psychiatric clinic about forty miles from where we lived. It was a hospital that specialized in children with behavioral problems, and to me it sounded like my very best chance of getting JP the help he needed. The downside, of course, was that I would have to commit JP for four or five months. He was still just a baby to me, and the thought of him locked inside a dreary hospital was horrifying — especially since I felt so responsible for what had happened to him.

Yet at the same time I knew I had to do something, and I just didn't see any other option. JP needed help — that was clear. And doctors at the clinic assured me they had dealt with children like JP before, and that they would give him what he needed most of all — a neuropsychological evaluation. If getting that help meant sending my son away to an institution for four months, what choice did I have but to do it? Just a few months before JP's ninth birthday, I arranged for him to go in for treatment at the clinic.

The day I dropped him off is one I will never forget. I stayed with him while a nurse drew blood, and I held his hand as we made our way to the children's wing. After a few minutes, a staffer made it clear it was time for me to go. I bent down and squeezed JP as tightly as I could, and I kissed him and told him over and over, "I love you." I don't think he understood what was happening, because he didn't say much — and that only made me hug him harder. Finally a nurse looked at me and mouthed the words, "Just go." I got up and walked away from my baby boy.

I told myself, *Don't turn around; just keep going.* Then I heard JP start to cry for me. "Come back, Mama!" he screamed through sobs. I knew I couldn't turn around, because that would only make it worse. Instead, with JP's cries echoing through the hall, I just kept walking. As soon as I turned the corner, I burst into tears.

That night in my suddenly quiet house I talked to a God I didn't know was listening.

"How long?" I asked Him. "How long is my son going to have to pay for my sins?"

A few months before I took JP to the psychiatric clinic, I'd resumed my college classes and entered the Teacher Education Program at a local university. My life had become a blur of appointments, classes, pickups, and drop-offs. Take the kids to day care, go to school, get the kids, go to work, get home, study, sleep, rinse, and repeat. I'll never forget the frantic feeling of being two hours late to pick up my children at day care one afternoon. I found them with a saintly teacher who bought them ice cream and stayed with them until I showed up. To this day, JP and Sabyre like to tease me about it. "Way to forget about us, Mom," they'll say.

Money, to say the least, was tight. I was only a step or two ahead of the bill collectors, and I'd usually have to drive down to the electric company to pay a bill just hours before my power got shut off. On one of those trips — when all I had to my name was $75 in the bank, enough to cover the bill I was paying — my trusty little red Eagle Talon went and exploded on me.

That's right, the engine literally exploded as I sat in the utility company drive-through, paying my bill. There was a crack in the engine, apparently, and I guess I was lucky I didn't crash. What did I do? What else? I laughed my head off. I certainly couldn't afford to get the car towed, much less fixed, so I had some nice people help me push it out of the drive-through. Then I called a scrap place and sold the smoldering wreck for $100. I remember taking all of my things out of the car and holding them while I waited for my mom to pick me up in the parking lot. My extra shoes and children's toys and books and dolls — you know, all the stuff of my life.

But life, as it does, went on, and eventually I did graduate. That was one of the proudest days of my entire life. No one had given me that diploma. I earned it with a lot of sweat and tears.

Right around the time my car exploded, out of desperation I'd applied for a job at an insurance office in town. I'd quit working at the country-western bar, because I couldn't stand being away from my kids at night. But I had to make money somehow, so when I heard about the insurance job, I jumped. I'd never learned to type, but my Grandma Ernie had encouraged me to take piano lessons. I guess my fingers were limber enough to bang out seventy words a minute on my typing test. My would-be boss, David, and I wound up being a perfect match: he was in desperate need of a secretary, and I was in desperate need of a job. He offered me the position, which came with a salary, steady income, and the chance to earn bonuses. Also, a normal schedule — no nights or weekends. It felt like I'd hit the jackpot.

I went to work in David's office, which was connected on one side to a donut shop. For the first couple of days, I loved the sweet smell of donuts in the air. By day three, and from then on, it made me kind of sick. A constant sugar rush, though, seemed like a small price to pay for a good, steady job.

But there was another problem. My first

week at work was also the week I had to take JP to the clinic. I was allowed to see him three days a week — two visits and one day of family counseling — but in order to see him I'd have to find a way to leave work early. And how could I ask my boss for time off from a job I'd only just started? But since I had no choice, I scrounged up my courage and asked David if I could work through lunch so I could leave at 4:00 p.m. and drive up to see my son. I was terrified he was going to fire me on the spot.

He didn't. He agreed to let me leave early three days a week. It turned out there were circumstances in David's life that allowed him to understand and sympathize with what I was going through. He said that sometimes it felt like his work at the office was the only thing holding his family together. That's why he was so kind to me — he knew I needed a helping hand, same as he did. Once I learned what he was going through, it made me want to work even harder for him and for the business. It was just the two of us, but we became a really effective little team. During my time at David's agency he won several awards, and I even won one myself for my work with children in the community.

But even better than the awards was the

friendship we developed. We helped each other through a really tough time for both of us. David became one of my dearest friends, and though he moved away, I still speak with him every now and then. I wonder if he knows that when he hired me, he basically saved my life.

Thanks to David, I went to see JP every chance I could (we also got to talk on the phone ten minutes a night, not nearly enough time for either of us). In my visits, I could tell his condition was slowly improving. They'd given him different mood stabilizers, and it seemed to be working. He was still having problems with many of his frontal lobe functions — inhibitions, emotions, impulse control — but at least we were getting some tools to help us handle it.

In the middle of this whirlwind called my life, a person appeared who changed everything. He wasn't someone I ever expected or even wanted to meet, and I fought as hard as I could to make him go away. But he wouldn't, and he didn't. And so my crazy little life took an amazing new turn.

Believe me, by then I was all but finished with men. I just didn't have time for games and drama, and after what had happened with Steven and JP, I was even more careful about who I brought into lives. Only many years later would I realize you aren't the only one in control of who enters your life. Sometimes greater forces are at work putting people in your path.

It started when a friend invited me for a glass of wine at the Air Force base. I was way too tired to go, but my friend was persistent. "Come on, one glass," she said. Sabyre was staying with my mom, and JP was still in the clinic. Reluctantly I went to meet my friend.

At the main gate, a guard stopped us and sent us into an office to get a pass. This guard, an older guy, started hitting on my friend and me in a really obnoxious way. You know, leering at us and making inappropriate comments. I had zero tolerance for bigmouthed men anymore, and I was just about to lay into him when another guard in the office suddenly spoke up.

"You going on a date or something?" he asked me.

I looked over at this other guard. He was sitting at a back desk eating Girl Scout cookies — Thin Mints, to be exact. He was a light-skinned black man about my age, and he had a beautiful smile and warm, friendly eyes. Right away I sensed there was nothing mean or threatening about him. He was the kind of guy who would have turned my head in years past, but I'd had more than enough of men clumsily hitting on me. He was just in the wrong place at the wrong time.

"That's none of your business," I snapped. "You don't need to know that to give me a pass, do you?"

The guard looked wounded. "I'm sorry, miss, I didn't mean it that way," he said. "I just think you look beautiful."

I didn't say anything else; I just took my pass and stormed out. A few hours later, in my friend's room, I began to feel bad about how rude I'd been. It wasn't like me to snap like that — well, not for no reason, anyway — and I wanted to apologize to the guard. I had my friend call the gate and tell him I was sorry. Instead, she invited him over. I was surprised an hour later when he showed up in full uniform.

I apologized for my rudeness, and we wound up sitting and talking for about four hours that night. If nothing else, this guy was a *great* listener. For some reason, I felt okay telling him about my kids and JP's accident and all that — not every detail, of course, but a pretty good overview. And he sat there with those warm, friendly eyes and let me tell my tale of woe. He didn't make a move on me or even try to kiss me, and at the end of the night he just gave me a peck on the cheek and said he hoped he'd see me again.

"You're going to marry him," my friend said as soon as he left.

"Oh, please," I said. "I'm probably never going to see him again."

Only much later would he tell me that he fell in love with me that night.

His name was Virgil, and he was a U.S. Army Security Forces officer stationed at the base. He was born in Texas, but when he was a child, the searing heat gave him skin rashes, so his parents moved him north to Oklahoma. His dad, Vernon, was a truck driver who steered giant rigs strapped with huge drums of dangerous chemicals, and Virgil knew him to be as tough a man as there was. One winter when the roads were iced over, his dad's truck slid into a deep ditch and toppled over. Luckily, he didn't seem too badly hurt, but he refused to go to the hospital to get an X-ray. He just went home all sore and bruised and spent the next few days picking tiny bits of the windshield out of his clothes. (He's come a long way since then; today, Vernon owns his own construction business in Oklahoma City.)

Virgil's mother, Eddie, met his father in college, where she was earning a psychology degree; family lore has it she did a lot of his homework for him. They were in their early twenties when Virgil was born, and they took him to their Baptist church every Sunday. After a while, though, they stopped going to church, and young Virgil stopped going, too.

But when Virgil was fourteen, his basketball coach, a deeply religious man, started talking to him about salvation — how it was possible for him to be saved in the eyes of God. Something about the concept of salvation really stuck with Virgil, and that year he entered into a relationship with God. There was no elaborate ceremony or ritual —Virgil just went off on his own somewhere and spoke a few words to God. "Lord, I am a sinner, and I ask you to forgive me my sins," he said. "I believe that you died on the cross for my sins, and I ask you now to enter my heart as my savior."

As Virgil would later explain it to me, that was the start of a long and beautiful process. From that day on, Virgil has never looked back. He has never doubted, not even for a moment, that God is real and lives in his heart. "I can trust God," he will say. "I know

He will help and protect me." In a nutshell, Virgil had the very certainty about God that I had always craved but never could feel. Where I went back and forth about God's existence and His goodness, Virgil never wavered. The presence of God was a plain and simple fact of his life, like the air he breathed and the food he ate and the grass that grew beneath his feet.

I had never met anyone like him.

So naturally, his first impression of me was "Wow, what a rude person."

Actually, Virgil didn't think that at all. He didn't let my rudeness bother him in the least. He wasn't a pushover or anything like that — far from it. He was a former boxer, and he was plenty tough, like his dad. But he was also kind and soft-spoken, and he always seemed like the calmest, most secure man in any room. Even so, I had no interest in dating him — I had no interest in dating, period. There was just too much going on in my life — and my track record with men was just too sorry — for me to get involved with anyone new. Virgil and I got together again for coffee a day or two after we met and went on to spend a lot of time talking on the phone, but I think I made it pretty clear I wasn't available. The best he could hope for was to become my friend.

And that is exactly what happened. Virgil seemed so interested in my problems and my struggles, and he always told me how strong I was and how much he admired me. I felt I was getting a very real measure of support from him at a time when I desperately needed it. For three or four weeks we'd sit around and talk and eat and watch movies, and I started to realize I'd never felt this kind of closeness with any other man in my past. Whatever it was that I was feeling, it felt *different.* It wasn't the head-over-heels passion and wild romantic yearning I was so used to experiencing. It was something deeper, more substantial — something that felt more *real.* After a month or so, I even decided to let Virgil meet my kids.

Sabyre met him first. She was only six years old at the time and had trouble pronouncing his last name — McVea — so she took to calling him Max. Well, Max and Sabyre became best pals. As gentle and generous as he was with me, he was even more wonderful with my daughter. Then one day I told Virgil I had to go visit JP in the clinic. He asked if he could come with me, but I didn't think it was fair to bring him in to meet JP in the institution, so I said no. Virgil said, fine, he'd come to keep me company, then sit in the car and wait while I saw JP. I told him the visit could last three hours. He said he didn't care.

So he drove with me and waited in the car for three hours while I saw JP.

Not long after that, I got a pass to take my son out of the clinic for a weekend. It was his birthday — he was turning nine — and I scheduled a whole day for us at the Omniplex, a gigantic science exhibition hall and zoo in Oklahoma City. Virgil called his parents, who lived in Oklahoma City, and told them his friend Crystal's son was having his birthday. His mother — demonstrating exactly where Virgil got his kindness from — opened up her house, invited all these friends and cousins, and threw JP his own birthday party, with a special cake and everything. It was just about the happiest I'd seen him in years.

By then it was clear to me I had real feelings for Virgil. It began to dawn on me that Virgil could be an important part of my life. My partner, my champion, my hero — someone who'd be there for me in a way no one else ever had. Not a day went by without Virgil telling me how beautiful I looked or what a great mother I was, and on some days I even allowed myself to believe him.

But on most days, my feelings for Virgil

were overwhelmed by a single, persistent thought: *He is too good for you.*

The self-hatred that had rooted in me since I was a young girl was, all those years later, part of me still. I wasn't the kind of woman good men like Virgil fall for. I didn't love myself, and I knew that God couldn't love me. So how could I accept someone like Virgil loving me? It couldn't be possible. It didn't make sense.

That's why I did everything in my power to chase Virgil away.

At some point I sat him down and listed every reason why he shouldn't be with me. I told him about the horrors of my childhood. I told him about the abortion. I told him how I had dated married men. I told him I had two children and how that was something he didn't want any part of. I gave him every reason under the sun to get up and walk away from me for good.

But Virgil didn't get up, and he didn't walk away. As I sat there crying and spilling my guts, he just leaned in and listened. When I was through, he spoke to me in that calm, reasoned way I was starting to get used to.

"You've earned a college degree," he said. "You work full-time and raise two great kids on your own. You have compassion for

184

people, and your humor and laughter draws them to you. You're one of the strongest women I've ever known. You have so many more good qualities than anything bad you can ever say about yourself."

And then he went in for the clincher.

"You survived all of that stuff," he said of my past, "and you have become the person I love."

A remarkable thing happened at that point — I stopped running.

But when I stopped running, everything I'd been running away from suddenly found me all at once.

And when that happened, the course of my life took its strangest turn yet.

CHAPTER ELEVEN

Virgil and I dated for several months before we decided to get married. The proposal? Well, Virgil didn't exactly propose to me, mainly because I didn't give him the chance. Once we knew we were going to be together, I vowed to do it right this time — no more living with someone and hoping it might work out. So when Virgil's stint in the Army was up and he got ready to become a civilian, I laid down the law.

"Either you need to get your own apartment or we need to get married," I said.

"Well," Virgil said with a wink, "I guess it's cheaper to marry you."

As much as I loved him, the idea of marrying Virgil scared me. My history with men was something I couldn't put behind me, and it was like I was always waiting for something to go wrong — only now it wouldn't just affect me. It would mess up my kids. When Virgil and I went to get our marriage license, I had a full-blown panic attack. I couldn't even sign the license, my hand was shaking so badly. Then I found I couldn't say the word "husband." The first time I heard someone refer to Virgil as my husband, I had another panic attack. To this day, we still laugh about that.

I guess this was just my mind playing tricks on me. In my heart, I knew I wanted to be with Virgil forever. When I told the kids we were getting married, they were beyond excited — they were already nuts about Virgil and had been for a while. So were my friends, and my mother, and everyone who knew him.

During my early twenties my life was so chaotic I went to church only sporadically, but after I met Virgil I became a regular churchgoer again. I even taught Sunday school at Grace Methodist Church — the same church I'd grown up in. Virgil and I decided to get married there after Sunday school. We both agreed we wanted a low-key affair. It was the second marriage for both of us, and we didn't feel we needed to have a big fairy tale wedding. We didn't invite many people — just my mom and my Aunt Bridget and uncle Al, my brother Jayson, and, of course, my children, plus a couple from the church who would be our witnesses. Virgil's parents, unfortunately, couldn't make it down from Oklahoma City.

We wanted the ceremony to be warm and informal, and it was. Virgil wore a simple white shirt and a nice pair of slacks, and I wore an autumn-colored skirt and a burnt orange sweater. That morning I'd gone to the store and bought some peach roses and peach-colored ribbon, and that was my bouquet. Simple yet beautiful. Sabyre and JP — who was out of the clinic and doing better — got dressed up in their Sunday finest and pranced around that morning like it was Christmas.

Right after Sunday school I told the nine teenagers in my class I was getting married. They were all so excited they stuck around to watch. It was like having our own little cheering section. The service itself took less than five minutes. The pastor, George, who was more like family to us than just a pastor, took us through our traditional vows — Do you take this man? Do you take this woman? — and then, just like that, we were married. Virgil leaned in and gave me a sweet little kiss, and all the kids, including my own, began whooping it up. During church service we have what we call a "thankful box," and if you want to share anything with the congregation, you just put a dollar in the box and start sharing. JP and Sabyre ran up and put a dollar in and yelled out their good news: "My mom and dad got married today!" they squealed.

And so I got my fairy tale wedding after all.

The honeymoon was a weekend in a fancy hotel in Oklahoma City — with the kids. They were at least as excited as we were and probably more. As soon as we got there, Sabyre helpfully told the receptionist, "We're on our honeymoon!" And once the hotel staffers knew, they sent a fruit and cheese plate and sparkling cider to our room. That weekend was one of the happiest weekends I've ever had.

You see, my marriage to Virgil brought something to my life that I never, ever had before: stability.

For the first time, I felt like I had solid ground under my feet. I got over my prewedding jitters and even started using the word "husband" freely (okay, so it took me three weeks into the marriage to stop referring to Virgil as "my boyfriend"). We bought a house in my hometown, and not long after that I got a new job teaching third grade at a local elementary school. JP was doing better, and both he and Sabyre loved their new dad. If life is a great big puzzle with a million tiny pieces, a lot of my missing pieces were starting to fall into place.

And yet I didn't react to my new stability like you might think I would.

Don't get me wrong. It was wonderful to have someone who loved me and was always on my side, and Virgil did indeed become my champion. He took over my fight to get JP on his dad's insurance and finally got it done. He helped me get JP in to see the specialists he needed. He made it so I didn't have to hustle quite as much as I had to when I was single. All my adult life I'd run around like a maniac from one job to the next, cleaning houses, ironing clothes, serving beers, finishing college, raising two kids, you name it. I don't remember ever slowing down. And all that working and running around made me lean and tough, if nothing else. I probably weighed less as an adult than I did as a student in high school.

But then, when I finally put down that burden — when I finally stopped running — I began to put on weight — and not just a little weight, but twenty extra pounds, then thirty. Before I knew it, I was more than fifty pounds overweight.

The real reason I got heavy, though, has nothing to do with working less. The truth is, once I stopped running from my problems and started putting down roots with Virgil, all the things I'd been running from just smashed into me all at once, like a chain reaction pileup on the highway. All my bad feelings about my abuse and abortion, all my fears and insecurities, all my guilt and self-loathing — it all just suddenly showed up together in my brain. I'd never really dealt with my problems; I'd just covered them up with anger, denial, avoidance, bad relationships, and long work hours. Basically, I'd just tried to outrun them. But now they finally got me standing still, and they overwhelmed me.

And so with my new outer stability came a new inner turmoil, if that makes any sense. I felt like I was always battling myself, always wrestling with my emotions. I know it sounds strange to say, but it truly felt like my mind and my heart were a battleground — only I didn't know who exactly was waging war.

At the center of this turmoil was my continuing confusion about God. It would have been nice if Virgil's certainty about God rubbed off on me, but it didn't. In a way, it only made me question God more. I tried to find God everywhere — in the beautiful rolling plains of Oklahoma, in the moody mountain sunsets, in the beaming smiles of my children.

"Virgil, look at that beautiful tree over there," I'd say, pointing to a magnificent elm. "God *had* to have made that. He has to be real, because all of this works so perfectly. There has to be a God!"

Patiently, Virgil would say, "There is."

But still I couldn't be sure. I truly wanted God to be real, but in my life I'd learned not to believe in anything I couldn't see with my own eyes. When Virgil came into my life, I started leaning toward the belief that God was real. But that was still a long way from truly believing. Much of the time I just didn't think He was listening to me. Whatever faith I had was kind of hollow. The truth is, I was still searching, still running — only now I was running toward something, not away from it. Because I needed Him more than ever, I was trying desperately to find God. "Come near to God," it says in James 4:8, "and he will come near to you." So, where was He?

It was then that God, who had never stopped trying, very clearly came near to me.

One of the first strange things that happened was a simple dream. And it involved my brother, Jayson.

Like me, Jayson was a headstrong little kid. He liked doing things his way, and he didn't like caving in to authority figures. I'll never forget what he did to my mom after she spanked him one day for not cleaning his room. He was nine or ten at the time, and he was so angry about the spanking that he cooked up an ingenious plan to get revenge. Back then my mom was working as a dental hygienist, so we always had a ton of dental floss in the house. Well, my brother took the floss and tied long strings of it to every single object in my mom's bedroom. I mean everything — tubes of lipstick, underwear in drawers, hairbrushes, shoes, the works. Then he tied all those strings around the doorknob of the bedroom door. It was a pretty heavy door, and to open it you had to give it a yank. So when my mom came home and pulled it open, everything she owned came flying at her and wound up in a big pile on the floor.

Jayson was waiting for her in the bedroom. Right on cue, he said, "Mom, your room's messy."

Jayson was in his early twenties when I got married to Virgil, and — like me in my early twenties — he was having a hard time with life. Everything we'd gone through as kids had left us battered and scarred. Only instead of turning to food or long work hours to treat the despair, he drank. And, unlike me, he wasn't struggling with the existence of God — he had a firm belief that God *wasn't* real. See, here's the big problem at the root of both our struggles. *If God was real and loving,* we wondered, *how could He have allowed what happened to us as kids to happen?* Why didn't He stop it? I wanted an answer to this question, but Jayson didn't need one. He didn't want anything from God at all. My brother flat out didn't believe that God was real, and he never let me talk about God around him.

Then, Jayson was arrested for driving under the influence for the second time. I lay in bed and asked God to help my brother. Before long, Jayson was facing his third DUI — and he hadn't budged an inch in his stance on God.

"God," I said during one of my prayers, "You're going to have to go get him, because he sure isn't coming to You. You're going to have to show Yourself to him, or he'll never believe in You."

One night, after just such a prayer, I had an incredible dream. I was in church — only I wasn't standing; I was hovering over the worshippers. I could see all these people on their feet with their hands in the air. They were singing and worshipping, and I had never seen people worship God like this before. It was a beautiful sight.

And in front, onstage, the person who was leading them in praise and worship was Jayson.

He is a great singer. As kids, we sang together all the time, and he's still a karaoke champ. And there he was, in my dream, arms raised and head thrown back, weeping out of sheer love for God and singing at the top of his lungs — singing praise to God! The guy who didn't believe God was real was leading a congregation in worship! When I woke up, the image of my brother seemed so real and so beautiful. It was more vivid than any dream I could remember having. I told Virgil and my mom about it, but I knew better than to tell Jayson. I just filed it away, and after a while I forgot it.

Then, in the summer of 2007, I had another powerful dream. This time, I was in my own bedroom, and once again I hovered high above it. I could see Virgil on his side of the bed, fast asleep, and I could see myself sleeping peacefully next to him. Then I became aware of this beautiful light encircling me as I hovered over the bed. The light began to outline this perfect plan for

195

our lives, and in my dream I soaked up each and every detail. I woke up and nudged Virgil and groggily said, "Wait until you hear God's plan for us." Virgil looked at me funny, because I'd never actually said I believed God was real, yet here I was telling him how God shared His plan with me. I drifted back to sleep, with every intention of telling Virgil every detail the next morning. But when I woke up, I couldn't remember what God had told me. I could only recall two odd and random things that seemed to have come from the dream: two numbers — *16* and *6* — and the image of building a great wall. I didn't know what any of it meant, and I chalked it up as just another weird dream. I mean, the only great wall I knew about was in China.

Those two unusually vivid dreams were just the start of this strange period in my life. What happened next was frightening, and I wish it had happened only in a dream . . . but it didn't.

Virgil and I had recently become friends with a young couple in town. They were a typical family — three beautiful children, a great house, all of that. I was very friendly with the wife. We talked a lot, and we had a really easy camaraderie. One summer night, shortly after my dream about the wall, Virgil and I went to dinner in their home. Afterward, the wife and I sat in their backyard talking about this and that.

By then, she had confided in me about her childhood. To my horror, what she described was even worse than my own history. She grew up in another state, and she told me that when she was just a kid, her mother joined a satanic cult and dragged her into it. She wound up being badly abused and raped by male members of the cult. The few details she shared with me were the stuff of nightmares. They seemed too horrible, too outrageous to be real. I did my best to console my friend and give her a sympathetic ear, but deep down I don't think I really believed her story. Or maybe what she described was just too evil for me to comprehend. On some level, I was still that terrified little girl who ran out of that sewing room thinking she had met the devil. I didn't know if Satan was real, but I didn't know that he was not. And I didn't want to believe what my friend told me, because if it was true, that would mean the devil could very well be real.

When she confided all that to me, she also said that once her friends knew about it, they usually stopped being her friends. And, you know, I wanted to run away from her when she told me, too. But something inside me wouldn't let me leave her. I just couldn't turn my back on this wounded little creature. So I remained her friend.

That night, in her backyard, she seemed quieter than usual. Out of the blue, she asked me something she'd never asked before.

"Crystal, do you think God is real?"

Of all the people in the world to ask.

I wasn't sure what to say to her, so I told her about my dream. Then I told her how I was searching hard for God and how my faith was slowly growing. She sat silently for a while, then asked another question: "Do you think God could love *me*?"

I don't know why I said what I said next; it just rolled out of my mouth without stopping at my brain first: "Do you want me to pray with you?"

I'd never personally prayed over anyone in my life. I mean, sure, I'd prayed *for* people in church, but I'd never laid hands and prayed *over* someone, like I'd seen people do in charismatic churches I'd visited. After all, who was I, the skeptic, to pray over anyone? My friend nodded her head and started crying, so I took her hand and started to pray. She bowed her head and listened, but before I was done, she suddenly lifted her head and looked straight at me.

What I saw startled me.

Her expression had gone from sadness to something that looked like anger. She had this hardened glare, like she'd just sucked on a lemon, but about ten times worse than that. She looked hateful and frightening. She began to laugh at me, but it was a laugh unlike any I'd ever heard. It was this cruel and unsettling cackle. Then she began mocking me and mocking the name of Jesus in a high-pitched, evil-sounding voice. I sat there thinking, *What is going on? What is wrong with my friend?*

Her husband, who had joined us earlier, was just as shocked as I was to see how she was acting. Now, she had been diagnosed with multiple personality disorder, a result, her doctors believed, of her childhood trauma. Sitting there, listening to her evil laugh, I put two and two together and turned to her husband.

"Is this one of her personalities?" I asked.

"No," he said. "I've seen them all, but I have never seen this."

I ran inside the house and found Virgil. "I don't know what I did, but I did something to her!" I said. Instantly Virgil sprang into action. He ran outside and up to my friend, who was on her feet and still ranting and raving in that strange, childish voice. He put her in a bear hug from behind and began talking in her ear. "Tell me your name," he said over and over while she spit out curses. "I will not listen to you until you tell me your name." I couldn't wrap my mind around what was happening. I was watching the poor woman go crazy, and it broke my heart. I was also confused why Virgil was speaking to her that way. Meanwhile, she just kept on urgently screaming my name — not Virgil's, not her husband's, just mine. I took a few steps back and tried to catch my breath. Honestly, I was scared to death. I didn't know what to do or what to say, but I knew I wanted the madness to be over.

In a tiny mutter under my breath I started repeating the name of Jesus.

Suddenly she stuck out her head and looked right at me with hatred in her eyes. She broke free of Virgil and lunged at me, but stopped just before she touched me, almost as if she'd hit an invisible wall. Then in a low but clear voice that was not her own she said, "Where's your Jesus now? You got what you deserved as a child."

I hadn't told my friend about my childhood abuse. I hadn't told anyone except Virgil. My first thought was that Virgil must have told her. I started crying, and Virgil told me to go home. I got in the car and drove home and locked all the doors and windows. Virgil came home a while later, and I hugged him tight when he walked in.

"She's crazy," I said. "She is nuts. We need to get her some help."

"No," said Virgil quietly. "I don't think that was her."

Virgil told me he reacted the way he did — quickly and forcefully — because he recognized what was happening as demonic. He was commanding what was inside her to say its name, so that with God's authority he could make it leave.

I stood there, more confused than ever, not knowing what to think. My husband was a smart and serious man; in all the time I'd known him he'd never told a lie or even exaggerated anything. He was as plainspoken and honest as a person could be. And here he was telling me our friend was possessed? What was I supposed to say to that?

Virgil told me she returned to her normal self after I left. She didn't remember anything that had happened, and she was deeply frightened when her husband and Virgil told her about it. It chilled me to the bone to think all of her venom had been directed squarely at me. I asked Virgil if he had told her about my childhood abuse, and he said he hadn't. I believed him, but that meant I had no idea how my friend knew what she knew.

That night I insisted we sleep with all the lights on. I jumped at every sound and lay in bed crying until the sun came up. To say I was terrified doesn't really convey what I was feeling. All I knew for sure was that my friendship was over.

The next day I told my Aunt Connie about what happened. Without hesitating, she said what I described was a demonic event. I knew the Bible talked about demons, but the truth is I hadn't read the whole Bible, only small parts of it. And no one had ever talked about demons in any church sermon I'd ever heard. I listened to what my aunt had to say, but deep down I had already convinced myself that what I saw was either part of the poor woman's personality disorder or evidence she was just plain crazy. Still, when Connie gave me the number of a Christian counselor she knew, I agreed to call him to ask if he could help. I didn't want to be around my former friend anymore, but I also didn't want her to suffer. If I could direct her to the help she needed, I would.

I called the counselor and told him everything that happened, and when I was done, he had one question. "She only said these things about you?" he asked.

I said yes, that was true, and the counselor paused.

"Then you're the one I need to talk to," he said.

Sorry, not interested, good-bye.

After that, I tried to let the matter drop, but I couldn't shake a sense of lingering dread and anxiety. For days I couldn't even be alone. Virgil had to sit with me in the bathroom while I showered, and in bed I'd get as close to him as I possibly could. Was all of this real? Was any of it real? It was easier for me just to believe she was crazy, and that's what I tried to do.

At this point, some of you might be saying, "Now hold on just a minute." Some of you might believe in demons; some of you may not. I am not here to tell you what to believe or what not to believe. All I can do is tell you the truth of my story, even if some of it is hard to fathom.

For me, the easiest explanation only held up for so long. How did she know about my past? Was it a guess? It seemed too specific for that. Had I forgotten that I'd told her? I was pretty sure I hadn't. And why was Virgil so sure he'd seen demonic influence? Didn't his opinion as a man of deep faith and strong character carry a lot of weight? All of these questions swirled in my head, but even so, I might have sided with the skeptics and forever believed what I'd witnessed was just a case of mental illness.

I might have believed that . . . if it hadn't happened again.

A few months had passed since we ended our friendship with the couple. I'd returned to my normal life, or as normal as I could get it. I taught school. I watched my kids play in the school band. I made them lunches and put notes on their napkins telling them how much I loved them. I didn't need to sleep with the lights on anymore, and — after not praying for weeks out of fear and confusion — I'd even started to pray again. Most evenings in our house were quiet, just the way I liked them.

On one of those evenings I invited a family friend to our home. She was a respected businesswoman and an all-around wonderful lady, and I was very close with her. I'd known her all my life, and she was down to earth and thoughtful and someone I considered a dear friend. I knew she didn't drink, but that night in my home she treated herself to one glass of wine. I didn't think anything of it, and our ordinary evening continued.

But within an hour or so, her mood changed. She started talking loudly and got very aggressive, and she said things she knew would upset me. My first thought was, *If she's drunk, I don't have time to babysit her. And I don't want my kids to see this, so I better drive her to her aunt's home,* which wasn't too far away. I called ahead, got my friend in my car, and we drove off.

On the way, she got even louder and meaner. At one point she grabbed the steering wheel, and I had to push her away and back in her seat. At her aunt's house, we sat her down in a recliner in the living room and let her cool down a bit. Instead, she only got more worked up. I'd never seen her act this way, and I could hardly believe a single glass of wine could cause it. She was staring at me now, just like my former friend had, with hatred in her eyes. And when she spoke she used a voice I didn't recognize as hers. Her uncle watched her and tried to make sense of her behavior, and her aunt was unnerved enough to grab a Bible and start reading passages aloud. And, just as it happened in the last incident, my friend started spitting the verses back in an ugly singsong voice. Then she started reciting the verses quickly, as if she knew them by heart, though I was sure she didn't know the Bible that well.

I felt a sickening knot in my stomach. One glass of wine could not explain all this. Her aunt kept reading the Bible, and she kept mocking her, until suddenly she stopped and looked straight at me.

Then she said something so vile and so brutal, I can't even repeat it in these pages.

Using horribly vulgar language, she told me I got exactly what I deserved as a child and she said she was responsible for all the horrible sexual abuse I'd suffered. It was like she felt proud of the hell inflicted on me when I was young.

I couldn't believe what I was hearing. The things she said cut me to my very core. How in the world did she know about my childhood abuse? Why would she use it as a weapon against me? I averted my eyes from her cold stare and looked straight at the wall and muttered "Jesus" under my breath.

That only made her cackle and mock me louder.

"Where's your Jesus now?" she spat out.

The blood drained from my face. She had used the exact same phrase. I might have been able to shrug off what had happened before, but now I couldn't — now it was happening again. I sat there absolutely terrified, but I put on a brave face and tried not to show my fear.

"I'm not afraid of you," I said, still looking straight ahead and avoiding her stare.

She leaped to her feet and lunged at me. She put her face inches from mine — so close I could feel her breath on my cheek — but she didn't touch me. Then she screamed: "YOU SHOULD BE!"

I got up and walked out of the house and drove home. I found Virgil in the living room.

"Call the hospital," I told him. "I need to be admitted to a psych ward. I think I'm losing my mind."

However you feel about demons, they are part of the wide-ranging conversation about God and faith in our world today. The Bible talks about demonic possessions, and there are several documented cases of possession throughout the history of Christianity. Even someone as mainstream as Bobby Jindal — the governor of Louisiana and a rising political star on the national stage — has written about witnessing a demonic attack while he was a student at the campus ministry University Christian Fellowship.

"Suddenly, Susan emitted some strange guttural sounds and fell to the floor," Jindal wrote of a fellow student in a 1994 article titled "Beating a Demon: Physical Dimensions of Spiritual Warfare." "She started thrashing about, as if in some sort of seizure. I refused to budge from my position and froze in horror. I will never forget the first comprehensible sound that came from Susan; she screamed my name with such an urgency that the chill still travels down my spine whenever I recall this moment." Later, "Susan proceeded to denounce every individual in the room, often citing very private and confidential information she could not possibly have known on her own. It was information capable of hurting individuals — attacking people, as she did, by revealing their hidden feelings, fears, and worries."

Sound familiar?

I told Virgil what happened and begged him to have me committed. I truly, truly believed I was going crazy. Even though other people had been there when these incidents happened, I simply couldn't think of any other explanation. The alternative — that I was being spiritually attacked — was just too far-fetched for me to believe. It was much easier to think I was losing my mind.

It didn't help when, a few days later, I

asked my friend's aunt why she hadn't stopped her from speaking to me the way she did. Her aunt said, "What way? All I heard was gibberish." Both her aunt and uncle were right there with me in the living room, as shocked as I was by what was going on, but they didn't hear her say those horrible things to me? How could that be? Had I misheard? Or was I really losing my mind?

Only many years later would I realize why I'd heard those things — and why, when I invoked the name of Jesus, it only made whatever was inside her attack me more. I was like someone who is home alone when a burglar breaks in. I grab a shotgun and confront the burglar, but he can see I'm holding the gun backward and my arms are shaking and my finger's not on the trigger. And maybe I even say, "I've never shot a gun before, but I will now!" The burglar knows I won't be able to defend myself against him. He sees the fear — he sees I have no *authority* over him. And so he steps up his attack.

Virgil, as he always does, sensed how truly terrified I was and calmed me down. He told me I wasn't crazy, that what I had seen was Satan at work. He talked about Satan as if he was talking about a next-door neighbor — matter-of-factly, without fear or drama. None of what was happening was too hard for Virgil to believe. And because he had the benefit of being certain about his beliefs, he wasn't a terrified, quivering mess like me.

I allowed Virgil to talk me out of the idea that I was crazy, but once again I insisted we sleep with all the lights on. I'd drift off with Virgil holding me and wake up terrified and drenched in sweat. I made sure I was never alone in any room for the next several weeks. And I swore to secrecy everyone who had witnessed these events. I didn't want anyone talking about them again, ever. I was a schoolteacher and a mom, and we were a good family — a *normal* family.

Worst of all, I stopped talking to God. I was simply too afraid to pray. I was afraid that if I began to pray, the attacks would happen again. What I did do was call the Christian counselor I'd spoken to previously. We made an appointment, and I drove to see him in a nearby town. On the way I felt scared to be in the car by myself, so I rolled down all the windows and blasted Christian music on the radio the whole way. I didn't usually listen to this type of music, but I figured it couldn't hurt.

The counselor was a pleasant man in his

fifties, with a calm demeanor that reminded me of Virgil. I sat across from him in his drab office and told him everything that had happened. He listened with no expression, betraying nothing, and when I was done, we sat in silence for a long minute.

"I am going to tell you what God has told me about you," he finally said. "What you are frightened of is demonic. And it is attacking you — specifically you."

I sat there absolutely stunned. How had my life taken such a strange turn?

"What do I need to do?" I asked. "Is there something you can give me?" I was hoping he had some special prayer or oil that would make it all go away.

"I'm not going to do anything," the counselor said. "God is going to help you fight this off. God has told me He is raising you up to be a warrior. And God is going to send you into the world to fight for others."

My only thought was, *I guess God doesn't know me very well.*

On the drive home I blasted the Christian music station again. A song came on about a man who was trapped by demons and calling out for help. He looks up and sees Jesus standing right in front of him, and the demons shriek and scurry away. The lyrics go, "Lift your chains I hold the key / All

211

power on Heaven and Earth belong to me."
I remember being surprised the demons had
fled in fear of Jesus. Why hadn't that happened with me? Was it because Jesus wasn't
there with me?

I don't know how to explain it, but when
I heard those lyrics, I got the powerful feeling that God was speaking to me. It wasn't
that I heard His voice in the lyrics; it was
more like I received a message *through* the
whole song. And what I heard God saying
over and over was, *"Did you not think I was
strong enough?"*

That night I started talking to God again.
The conversation was distilled into a simple
prayer. I asked for an answer to the question that was haunting me.

Was He real, or was I insane?

It had to be one or the other. Either what
was happening to me was real or I was going out of my mind. Either there was a God
and an adversary or I was a lunatic.

Which was it? I needed to know. God gave
me no immediate answer, so I kept praying
and living in fear and hoping that maybe
one day He would.

Then He did, more than once, only I
wasn't paying attention.

This is my dad, Brad, and my mom, Connie, in 1975, the year they got married.

My mom and me on Christmas Day 1979. I was three years old and ready to open more presents.

I was three when my stepdad took me fishing and I caught my first fish! He wasn't exactly thrilled that I caught more than he did.

That's me in my tomboy phase when I was three. My mom tried to get me to wear dresses, without much luck.

This was the day I got all dressed up for a playdate that never happened. At least I had fun blowing dandelions.

It was always a great day when Grandma Ernie and Paw Paw came for a visit. Here they are with me and my brother, Jayson, in 1982.

Me and three-month-old Jayson in our backyard in 1982. Look at that mischievous little grin!

The first day of school for Jayson (kindergarten) and me (fifth grade) in 1987. We got new backpacks and lunchboxes every year.

My dad in his Corvette dropping me off after one of our visits. I loved my time with him; he was the coolest guy I knew.

Dinner at my aunt's house: (from left) Jayson, my mom, Uncle Al, Aunt Bridget, Maude Marie (a family friend), and me.

Sweet Sixteen: here I am at a friend's house in 1993, one of my wild teenage years.

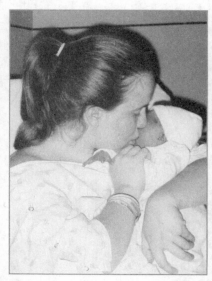

My son JP at eighteen months in these silly fake ears he loved wearing. What a little rascal he was.

This is the moment I met my son JP right after he was born in 1995. It was love at first sight.

In between my two jobs I'd rush home to be with my daughter Sabyre (she's six months old here).

Me with my daughter Sabyre and JP in 2001, when we were a happy family of three.

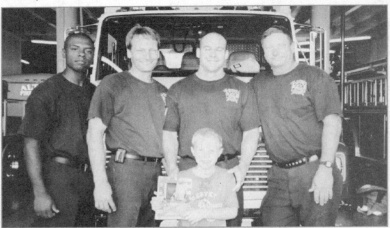

Here's JP with the firemen who saved his life after his accident in 2002. We brought them a framed photo of JP to thank them, and they gave him a firehouse tour.

My dad, Brad, came down from Illinois to be with me the day I graduated from college in 2003.

Virgil and me on our first date in 2004. His integrity and faith in God still inspire me every day.

January 30, 2005—the day Virgil and I got married in a Sunday school classroom. Our dear friend Pastor George Lupton officiated, and Sabyre and JP got all dressed up.

Virgil let Sabyre give him a makeover—and paint his toenails to match his lipstick!—in 2005. He is such a good dad.

Virgil and his parents, mom Eddie and dad Vernon. He sat on her lap, because he says he's still her baby.

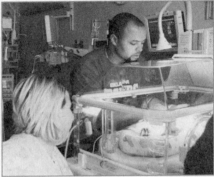

This is the moment I first laid eyes on my daughter Willow in the hospital NICU in 2009. She was 10 hours old and weighed 2 pounds.

My tiny burrito: I'll never forget this moment when I first got to hold my son Micah.

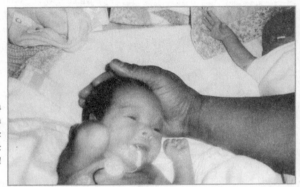

Little Willow didn't let a feeding tube stop her from giving us her very first smile. We waited for that smile for weeks!

After ten weeks in the hospital, we're finally going home! That's Virgil carrying the twins and their apnea monitors in 2009.

My daughter Willow on her first birthday in 2010. To think I almost missed this special day.

Virgil and me with the kids not long after the twins came home. We took this picture in July 2009, just four months before I died. (*Photograph by Amy Hart*)

My friend Patricia's lovely daughter Heather, with her floppy-eared bunny. Her grandparents still raise rabbits in her memory.

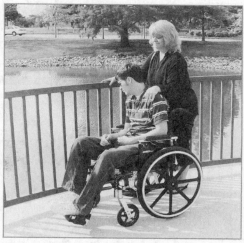

My friend Shearl and her son Mickey by the hospital pond where she prayed for his recovery every day. God was listening!

My brother, Jayson, and his beautiful wife, Melissa. I am just so happy they found each other.

Here's Brandon and Amber with Sabyre on the day she was baptized in a lake near our home in 2012. I love that crazy couple!

My big happy family at home. I thank God every day for the blessings He's given me.

Chapter Twelve

The place where God finally tracked me down wasn't a church or a school or a hospital or anyplace you might think.

It was a Pizza Hut.

My daughter, Sabyre, had earned a free small pizza for winning a reading award at school, and we drove to the Pizza Hut to pick it up. While we were waiting, I ordered a diet Coke. Our sweet, elderly waitress brought over our check, which was for $1. Not a bad deal.

But as she handed it to me, I felt the nudge.

I call it a nudge, because I don't know what else to call it. Actually it was more like a really insistent thought. I didn't hear a voice in my head or anything like that; instead, this thought just popped in my brain and started flashing like a neon sign. Have you seen the movie *Ghost*? When Whoopi Goldberg keeps hearing Patrick

Swayze tell her to do something, and she's the only one who can hear it, and she's annoyed because she doesn't want to hear it? Well, that's a bit what this was like. I kept getting the nudge, clear and persistent.

Give the waitress a $100 tip.

I didn't know where it came from; I just knew it wouldn't stop. It made no sense to me, and it actually made me kind of mad. *A $100 tip on a $1 bill? Huh?* It's not like Virgil and I were rolling in dough. We were pretty much going from paycheck to paycheck at that point. One hundred dollars was an absolute *fortune* for us. But the nudge was getting stronger, and I felt so overwhelmed, I went outside and walked around the parking lot. I called Virgil at work and told him what was going on.

"That's God," he said calmly. "Do what He's asking. I can't talk now, babe, gotta go."

But there was just no way I was going to leave a $100 tip. Then another thought asserted itself: *Okay, then leave $50.* My nudge, it seemed, was flexible. Honestly, I felt like I was on the fast train to Crazytown. I went back in and paid the bill and left a $10 tip — and even *that* struck me as too much.

But when I got in my car, the nudging

only got worse. Whatever it was that was all over me wasn't going away. I was being reminded that I hadn't done what was asked. I called Virgil again, and he said, "Babe, I'm in a meeting. I really can't talk. Go to an ATM and get the other $40 and take it to her. Bye." What kind of husband supports his nutty wife giving money away to strangers? I sat there thinking, *Gee, Virgil, thanks for nothing.* There were a million reasons why I couldn't leave such a generous tip. The utility bill was due. We needed new curtains in the bedroom. JP and Sabyre were owed their allowance. Why would I give a stranger money I didn't have?

And yet — the nudge. It wouldn't go away. Believe it or not, I called Virgil again.

"Just do what God is asking you to do," he said. No anger, no judgment, just calm, decisive advice.

Virgil knew we didn't have much extra money, but he didn't care. This was not his decision to make. This was God's decision. Or at least that's how he saw it. For me, it still seemed like lunacy. And yet I couldn't get myself to turn the ignition and drive away.

Instead, I took Sabyre by the hand, marched over to an ATM, and withdrew $40. I stomped back toward the Pizza Hut, angry at the whole situation. I thought, *Well, at least this will make me look like a really great person.* Which is when yet another thought pushed its way through my brain.

Tell her who this is from.

By that point, I not only felt like I was losing my mind, but I probably looked it, too. I was arguing with myself all the way to the Pizza Hut. "Great, so not only do I have to give my money away, but you want me to walk in and say, 'Oh, hi, this is from God'?" I wanted to turn around so badly, and yet I walked back in and spotted our waitress near the cash register. I took a deep breath and said, "Okay, let's get this over with."

The waitress seemed confused to see us.

"Hi, I gave you a tip earlier, but it wasn't the right amount," I said.

The waitress dug into her apron and tried to give me the $10 bill.

"No, no, that's not it," I said. "I gave you too little." Then I handed her the $40 in cash and said, "God asked me to give this to you."

She looked at me and said, "What?"

Naturally, she was hard of hearing.

"God asked me to give this to you," I repeated, loud enough to draw stares from staffers and customers. I could feel my face flushing the color of tomato sauce.

The waitress looked at the money in her hands and seemed completely stunned. Finally, after a few moments she screamed, "Oh, my God!"

"Yes," I said, "exactly."

I grabbed Sabyre and got out of there, feeling agitated and confused. I was not a cheerful giver, that's for sure. That night and the next day, I thought a lot about what happened and tried to make sense of it, and when I couldn't, I just tried to forget it. But three days later, as I was dismissing my students for recess, I got a call from Virgil. The first thing he said was, "You need to sit down."

My first thought was, *Oh great, he got fired, and I just gave away $50.* But that wasn't it. "I happened to walk in on a conversation with the guy who manages that Pizza Hut," Virgil told me. "He was talking about this lady who came in and gave a waitress a fifty-dollar tip. I said, 'That was my wife.' "

It turns out the waitress's husband had just lost his job, and they couldn't afford to have their two children join them for Thanksgiving. So she prayed to God to somehow let her earn the $100 she needed on her last shift. By the end of her shift, she'd made only $50. Her kids would not be joining her for Thanksgiving.

And then, of course, I walked in — her very last customer. And she got to bring her children home.

When I heard this story, I was dumbfounded. There was no way this could be just a coincidence. "You have to be real," I told God. "There's no other explanation." I finally had the proof I'd been searching for all those years. God, wouldn't you know it, *was* real. That feeling filled me with a huge sense of relief and joy.

Or at least it did for the next three or four days.

After that, whatever sureness I felt slowly faded away. I couldn't convince myself this was how God worked — by nudging people in Pizza Huts. I went back to thinking it had all been a big, annoying coincidence.

And just like that, I let God slip through my fingers.

When I think back on that incident now, I can see how incredibly patient God was with me. Over and over He spoke to me, and over and over He answered my prayers and gave me proof of His existence, and every time I chalked it up to coincidence. God even used me to answer someone else's prayers, and instead of acknowledging that, I gave myself a nice little pat on the back for my good deed — when in fact it had nothing to do with me. Truth be told, I wasn't even completely obedient to God when I left that tip. The Pizza Hut waitress had prayed to make $100 that day, and in the end she did, and she praised God for answering her prayer. *But,* God didn't want me to just match her $50 that day. He had asked me to give her the entire $100. He wanted to go *above and beyond* for the child He loved. He wanted to give her *more* than what she'd asked for. I believe that sometimes God wants to bless us beyond whatever blessing we pray for. And sometimes what stops that from happening is us.

Through all of the dreams and scares and nudges, one thing was constant — my wonderful husband, Virgil. He was always a rock of support for me, and he knew how to defuse the drama that seemed to swirl around my life. He never got tired of all my questions about God — and he never tried to overwhelm me with his own beliefs. He just shared his incredibly strong convictions and waited patiently for me to come around.

We'd been married for almost five years when, out of the blue, I cornered Virgil in the kitchen and asked him a question.

"If it were possible," I said, "would you

want to have a child?"

Me having a child with Virgil wasn't all that simple. The fact is, after Sabyre's birth, I had a tubal ligation — which means your fallopian tubes are tied off and you can't have any more kids. I did it, because I couldn't handle another pregnancy that wasn't part of a sound and loving relationship — and there weren't too many of those floating around in my life. Virgil knew going into our marriage that I couldn't have kids. He loved me enough to marry me anyway.

But now I was feeling guilty that I couldn't give him a child. I could see what an amazing father he was to JP and Sabyre, and it pained me to think we couldn't have a son or daughter of our own. I mean, JP and Sabyre were his kids in every way, except he didn't get to experience the whole process with them — the birth, the early years, all of that great stuff. One day after brushing my teeth, I sat on the edge of the bathtub and started talking to God about it.

"God, I know I don't deserve another child," I said, "but please do not punish Virgil for what I've done. He is such a wonderful father."

This was the start of a series of bargains I made with God, a string of tests through which He could prove to me that He was real. I wanted to believe — I was *leaning* toward believing — but I was still a long way off from actually believing. I was the ultimate skeptic, demanding proof, setting conditions, challenging God. I don't know what made me think I was in any position to do this. It wasn't like God owed me something — in fact, it was me who sinned greatly against Him. Still, in our conversations, I set up hurdle after hurdle. The Pizza Hut nudge had been forgotten.

Within a week of that little bathroom prayer, I got a random e-mail at work from a fertility clinic in Oklahoma City. I knew we couldn't afford the fee — it was something like $35,000 — but since the first appointment was free, I scheduled one anyway. At the clinic, the doctors were kind and wonderful, but they told us they accepted only a few patients at a time and were completely booked for the next few months. Oh well, another disappointment — no big deal. Virgil and I were halfway out the front door when I heard someone say, "Wait."

Incredibly, sometime during our appointment, another couple had canceled and the slot was ours if we wanted. Not only that, but the fee was drastically less than I'd first believed. If we scrimped and saved, we might be able to afford it. Virgil and I looked at each other, and a big smile crept across his face. We both knew what we were going to do.

The next few months were full of shots and tests and visits to the clinic. The idea was to harvest eggs and sperm and create an embryo in the lab. The embryo would be monitored in the lab for a few days before it was implanted in my uterus. We actually got to see pictures of the eggs dividing in a lab dish. We took to calling the fertility specialists our babysitters.

Finally, after several weeks, I was implanted, and after that I had to go home and lie down with my feet up for two weeks before I could find out if I was pregnant. There were no guarantees, and I knew many women went through fertility treatments for years without success. Those few days after I was implanted were agonizing. Not surprisingly, I had another little talk with God.

"If You're real," I said, "then I will be pregnant."

Just one day shy of two weeks, I couldn't wait any longer. They wanted me to go to the clinic to take the pregnancy test, so they could be there to counsel me if it was negative. But I just couldn't delay it another second. I got a home pregnancy test and locked myself in the bathroom. I looked at the strip and waited for a symbol to emerge.

And then it did — a small, simple plus sign.

I called my fertility doctor and asked if a positive result on a pregnancy test could be wrong. He told me there were no false positives, only false negatives. That was it, then — I was pregnant.

I was pregnant!

A bit later Virgil found me in the living room, and casually I told him, "Oh, we're pregnant" — as if I were talking about a bag of groceries I'd left on the counter. I have this thing where I sort of shut down when I get too excited — I guess it's some kind of defense mechanism. There are plenty of times when I lose my cool, but other times, when you might expect me to be jumping out of my skin, I'm completely calm and collected, in a world of my own. This, strangely, was one of those times. Virgil, on the other hand, lost it. He hugged me and kissed me and told me he loved me and said, "I'm so, so happy."

A few days later I talked to God again.

"If it's twins," I said, "*then* I'll know You're real."

After a blood test confirmed I was pregnant, we went in for an ultrasound. The nurse tilted the monitor so we could get a better look at the miracle inside me. After a minute or two, she spotted something and said, "Okay, there's your baby." My heart sank for a moment, but then I was grateful that at least one of the embryos had made it. And then the nurse said, "Wait — there's baby number two." I covered my face with my hands and started crying.

Virgil looked at the nurse and said, "Okay, you can stop counting now."

The next bargain I made with God was about the gender of my babies. "If it's a boy and a girl, then I will know You're real." At fifteen weeks, an ultrasound showed I was having a boy and a girl. Incredibly, my bargaining with God wasn't over. "If one has green eyes and the other has blue eyes, then I'll know You're real." I know, ridiculous, right? Somewhere along the line, I even asked God to help me find an affordable van with low miles and a DVD player for the kids. The first car dealer told me we would never find one that met our price. At the second lot, we found it.

"Come on, Virgil, that's just a coincidence," I said. "People get deals on cars all the time."

"God is answering your prayers, and you still don't believe it's Him," Virgil said.

When I told a friend of mine how receptive God seemed to be to my prayers, she said, "Would you mind asking God for a couple of things for me? 'Cause I've never seen anyone ask for stuff and get it like you do."

And still, what I wanted most of all I didn't have. What I wanted most of all was to believe.

And then, when I was just twenty-five weeks along, I felt a sudden, blinding burst of pain in my stomach.

Virgil rushed Me to the doctor, who told us my body was trying to go into labor. He gave me a shot of terbutaline to stop my contractions. It did the trick, and the doctor prescribed bed rest and sent us home. For the next month I lay around, caught up on all my TV shows, and watched my tiny babies move around in my tummy. Everything was fine, until the day Virgil started retiling the kitchen floor. Before he started he asked, "Honey, are you sure you're okay? This is going to take a while." I assured him I was fine and told him to get to work. He slipped on his kneepads and began digging up grout.

Well, no sooner had he flipped his first tile than I said, "Uh, I think I need to go to the hospital." I'd been fighting off mild cramps earlier, but they just got stronger and more frequent, until one of them felt like I'd been kicked by a soccer player. "Crystal, I just started tiling!" said Virgil, but he didn't waste another second getting me to the hospital.

The doctors monitored me for a while, then let me go home again. But that very night, while Virgil was at Walmart picking up some tiling materials, I collapsed in the bathroom with the worst pain I've ever experienced. This didn't feel like a cramp or a contraction — this felt like something was seriously wrong. I called Virgil, and he raced home and drove us to the emergency room at close to 100 miles per hour. In the ER one of my waters broke. I was only twenty-nine weeks along.

My doctor called for an ambulance and sent us to the Oklahoma University Medical Center in Oklahoma City. Virgil couldn't ride in the ambulance with me, so he followed closely in the new Uplander van I'd prayed for. The pain was getting worse, and the paramedic sitting beside me in the ambulance kept talking to me in a soft, low voice to try to keep me calm.

"All I need is something for the pain," I

told him. "Please give me something for the pain."

"I'm sorry. We don't have any pain meds in the ambulance," he said.

"What kind of ambulance doesn't have something for pain?!" I screamed.

The ride to Oklahoma City was endless. We hit road construction a couple of times and had to be detoured. Then we took a wrong turn somewhere. At one point I remember yelling, "I'm going to have these babies right here!" The ambulance guys were sweet and kept assuring me I was okay. "How many babies have you delivered," I yelled out, "because you're going to deliver mine." The paramedic closest to me said, "I helped deliver one baby."

"None," said the driver, "cause I drive *fast.*"

Still, traffic is traffic, and we were still a ways from the hospital. The pain cascading through my body was only getting worse. I heard my cell phone ring, and it was Virgil, calling from the van behind us. He told me he loved me and that everything was going to be okay. I wished I could believe him, but I knew something was terribly wrong with me.

Then my cell phone rang again. With the pain ripping away at my insides, I managed a faint hello. It was a friend of mine calling to chat.

"You're not going to believe the day I'm having," she said.

For some reason, I listened to her tell me about her day. Maybe I was shutting down, like I do in moments of emotional crisis. I think she got a parking ticket, or maybe her dry cleaning was lost. After a few minutes I finally said, "Okay, well, I'm in an ambulance, so I gotta go."

We finally made it to the hospital and in to see a doctor. He immediately put me on a magnesium drip to slow down the contractions. I was dilated only one centimeter, not the ten I needed to be to deliver my babies. The doctor said he wanted to keep me in the hospital for at least six weeks, so I could reach the thirty-five-week mark. That meant Virgil would have to take time off from work, but what else could we do? I got my mother to watch the children, and we settled in for the long haul.

Yet no matter what the doctors did, the pain just wouldn't go away. It only got more and more intense. I kept telling everyone, "Something is wrong, something is wrong," but the doctors kept saying it was just premature labor. It got to the point where after every single contraction I'd scream at the top of my lungs. I remember Virgil's utter frustration and him laying his head on my stomach one night and just weeping. He kept badgering the doctors to find out what was wrong and so did I, but nothing anyone did made the pain go away.

Finally, one of the contractions was so horrible, I screamed until I couldn't scream anymore. My mother, who was visiting, watched the color drain from my face. Then she looked at the floor beneath my bed.

It was covered in blood.

Nurses and doctors scrambled into the room. Someone yelled a Code something. I saw Virgil slipping on scrubs before they wheeled me out of the room. I remember hearing someone say, "Knock her out," and I remember the mask coming down on my face, and then I don't remember anything else.

The next thing I knew, I was back in my hospital room, and Virgil was standing over me. I was groggy and confused, and it took me a moment to realize I didn't know if my babies had made it or not. I looked at Virgil's face for any sign of grief or panic. I couldn't bring myself to ask the question.

"Everything is okay," Virgil said. "The babies are here. They're really little, but they're here."

There had been something wrong with me after all. The pain I felt wasn't only contractions. I'd had a placental abruption, which meant the placental lining was ripping away from my uterus. The doctors figured they had plenty of time before I actually delivered, because I was still dilated only two centimeters when they checked. But I went from two to ten in under an hour, and those little babies were coming. Doctors panicked when they couldn't pick up one of the fetuses' heartbeats on a monitor and rushed me into surgery. The babies were delivered by cesarian section.

When Virgil said they were little, he wasn't kidding. The boy, who we named Micah, was only three pounds, and the girl, Willow, was just two pounds. When babies are born, they get an Apgar score, which gives you an idea of their health and vitality on a scale of zero to ten — with zero being all but dead. Willow was given a six. Micah got a one.

The curse of my family: our babies come out fragile.

They put our babies in separate incubators in the neonatal intensive care unit, or the NICU. It was only two babies per room, and they had a round-the-clock nurse. The second night they were there, we heard a loud siren go off in the hospital. Virgil and I looked at each other; we knew what the siren meant. It was a tornado warning. Tornados come out of nowhere in Oklahoma, and sometimes you have only a few minutes to find a safe place. We could hear the rain begin to crash against the windows. We had no idea what the hospital's tornado plans were, so we rushed to the NICU. The babies there were among the most vulnerable patients in the whole hospital, so the policy was not to move them unless it was absolutely necessary.

But then the sound of the rain outside grew louder, and all of a sudden water began leaking from the ceiling right onto Willow's incubator. Six nurses rushed in, frantically unplugged the incubators, and moved them to a drier spot. "This has never happened before," one of the nurses told us, and Virgil and I looked at each other and for some reason started to laugh. Like I said, we do that a lot in my family — laugh instead of cry. Our tiny twins were vulnerable enough without a tornado thrown into the mix. And yet here it was, raining *inside* the NICU. What else could we do besides laugh? Eventually the tornado moved on, the rain stopped, and the NICU went back to normal.

The very first time I laid eyes on the twins was a moment I'll never forget. It was a mixture of joy and horror at how small and fragile they were. My twins weren't any bigger than a flip-flop, and yet they were each hooked up to a million tubes and wires. They were so tiny, the smallest diapers available for preemies were *still* too big for them, and the diapers had to be rolled up and doubled over so they wouldn't swallow the twins whole. Both Micah and Willow had these minuscule blood pressure cuffs around their tiny wrists — cuffs so small they might not even fit around my pinky. Worst of all, the twins showed no signs of life. They didn't cry or wiggle or move their hands or legs at all. Their eyes never opened, and they didn't make a sound. We weren't allowed to hold them, but we could put our hands through a tube into the incubator and touch them that way. A nurse told us, "Just touch, don't rub, because if you rub you could rip their skin off."

The next few days were a nightmare. I begged the doctors and nurses to give us a prognosis, but no one would tell us anything concrete. I was looking for any little scrap of hope, but hospital staffers were careful to give us none. We heard things like, "We can't predict" and "It's too early to say" over and over again. Specialists came in and out, and still we had no answers. And so we looked for solace in even the tiniest sign of progress. "The first twenty-four hours are an important hurdle," one doctor told us, and we found great comfort in the fact that our twins made it to day two. A nurse assured us she'd seen even smaller babies in the NICU, and that made me feel a little better, even though I couldn't imagine babies coming any smaller than mine.

The area around the NICU became the center of our world. I still hadn't fully recovered from the pregnancy, so it was important for me to get rest. Still, I tried to be in and around the NICU as much as possible. Virgil and I occasionally snuck out to shower and grab a few hours' sleep in my brother's home in Oklahoma City where we were staying, but for the most part, we set up camp in the NICU. We weren't the only anxious parents there, and we got to know some other people who were also going through this ordeal. We'd see parents and relatives in the waiting room rubbing their tired eyes just like us, and we'd watch them get their scrubs on so they could go in and see their children.

Sometime during our second week, we saw a whole family go in together. We knew that if more than two people were going in to see a baby at once, it meant the baby was dying. They were crying and hugging each other, and I burst into tears just watching them make the short, sad shuffle into the room to say good-bye.

And that's when it hit me, right there in the NICU — *I am waiting my turn.*

The thought filled me with grief and sorrow, but I couldn't banish it from my brain. JP's accident had not been my punishment. No, *this* was to be my punishment. How long would it be before I, too, was pulling on my scrubs and shuffling in with my weeping family to say good-bye to my children? A day? Two days? A week?

And in that moment, ironically, my belief in God was stronger than it had ever been. Finally He seemed real to me — finally I believed. *Yes, God exists,* I thought. *And He is a punishing God.*

Around that time, both Virgil and I stopped praying for the twins to survive. In the early days, we both prayed constantly: Virgil in his quiet way and me in my unsure way. But then, we both stopped, for very different reasons. Virgil stopped because he decided to turn the whole situation over to

God. "I give this all to You," he told God around the second week. "Thy will be done."

Me? I stopped because I was tired of my conversations with God. At first I'd begged Him to spare my babies, but before long I resorted to threats. "If You take one of my babies, I will hate You forever," I said. "I will never, ever speak to You again." And then, after I had my realization in the NICU, the threats seemed pointless to me. God was going to do what God was going to do.

For the first twelve days we didn't get to hold Micah and Willow. We could reach into the incubators and help change their diapers or swap out their bedding, but that was it. Sometimes they barely seemed alive in their sterile incubators: no smiles, no sounds, nothing. Just two pale, tiny creatures, clinging to life.

Then, on day thirteen, a nurse came into the NICU and said, "Okay, are you ready for kangaroo time?"

The nurse explained the babies were strong enough for a little kangaroo care. That's when preemies are put on their mother or father's chest, skin to skin, for an hour or two. It's meant to give the child a sense of warmth and closeness with the parent, which is thought to help the baby but which *definitely* helps the parent. Neither Virgil nor I were expecting it, and we were happily shocked.

We sat in reclining chairs and waited for the nurse to bring the twins over. First she laid Micah on Virgil's chest. Then she took Willow out of her incubator and brought her to me. Just before she laid her on me, I panicked.

"I can't do it," I said. "She's too small. Please, I can't do it."

"It's okay," the nurse said. "Just give it a try."

She laid this little wisp of a thing on my upper chest, close to my neck. I gently put a hand on her tiny back — the first time I ever held my daughter skin to skin. I couldn't believe I was finally holding one of my babies, and I wiped tears off my face so they wouldn't fall on Willow. I held her for two hours like that, watching her body rise and fall with my every breath. She didn't do much besides sleep and maybe twitch here and there, but that was okay with me. I had her now, and during kangaroo time the terrible fear in my gut subsided.

It's true Willow didn't do much while I held her; she never even fully opened her eyes. But at one point, she *did* open them a teeny bit. And when she did, I took a quick look at her eyes; I did the same with Micah when I held him later that day.

And that's how I discovered that Willow had green eyes and Micah's eyes were blue.

THE QUESTION

In heaven, alongside God, all the questions I had for Him no longer needed answers. How could He abide evil in this world? Why was He such a punishing God? In His presence, I knew in an instant that God's plan for us is perfect, even when bad things happen and we don't understand why.

But I did have one question I felt compelled to ask, and as soon as I found myself in God's presence, I asked it: *Why didn't I do more for You?*

It wasn't a question as we know it; it was something that passed between us in that effortless, instant way. The same ease and fullness of communication I experienced with my angels was there with God, too. And because of that channel connecting us and allowing things to pass between us — and infusing me with more and more and more of His love — I felt humbled, and I felt compelled to address this shortcoming from my time on Earth. And I didn't just *ask* the question, like I might ask someone for the time — no, this was more of a profound and absolute surrendering of myself, a wrenching and overpowering admission of inadequacy. As if I were crying and throwing myself at His feet and pleading, with every fiber of my being, "Why? Why? Why didn't I do more for You? Why didn't I accomplish more in Your name? Why didn't I talk more about You? Why didn't I do what You asked me to do?"

It's not that I felt regret — regret is a negative emotion, and there is nothing negative in heaven — it's that I loved God so immensely I felt like He *deserved* so much more from me.

But God wouldn't allow me to feel bad about it. There is no feeling bad in heaven. There was no answer to my question, because there was no need for an answer. Despite what I had believed on Earth, I knew instantly that our God is not a punishing God. He is a loving God.

I realized I didn't just love God.

I realized He *IS* love.

Then the four of us — God, my two angels, and I — were moving down a tunnel. It was a magnificent passageway of blinding, swirling, shimmering brightness — brightness above me and on my sides. I have heard people who died talk about finding themselves in a tunnel, and I understand why they use that term — because, while it wasn't like any tunnel we have on Earth, it felt like the brightness was not only surrounding me but *guiding* me toward something. And at the end of the tunnel there was a burst of an even brighter light

— more intense and more vivid and more golden and more beautiful than all the other brightness.

And I instantly knew what this brightness was.

It was the gates of heaven.

I was at the very entrance to heaven.

And then an understanding passed between God and me. The channel that connected us was always open and we were communicating constantly and intensely, but this was a purer communication, a more important message.

The instant I became aware of the gates of heaven, God said, *"Once we get there, you cannot come back."*

I understood we were near the point of no return in my journey, and that filled me with such excitement and such expectation, I couldn't wait to get there.

But, in that same instant, I had a vision of my four children.

I'm not sure exactly how they appeared to me; all I know is they became part of my awareness. All four of them — JP, Sabyre, Micah, and Willow — so clearly came up in my mind, because I was nearing the point where I would not be able to go back and see them again on Earth.

But in the same instant that my children

came to me, I also understood that they would be okay without me, that, like He does for all of us, God had a perfect plan for their lives. I would see them again soon enough, there in heaven. It wasn't like I had this big argument with myself about it. I knew what I wanted to do. "Anyone who loves his father or mother more than me is not worthy of me," it says in Matthew 10:37. "Anyone who loves his son or daughter more than me is not worthy of me." I can remember hearing this scripture preached on Sunday mornings and thinking, *I could never love anything more than my children.* I simply couldn't fathom it. But in this perfect moment, a moment God created for me, I understood, and I was absolutely clear about my intentions. I knew there could be nothing between God and me. God comes first, and everything else is second. And so another understanding passed between us.

"I want to stay with You," I said.

We moved through the tunnel, toward the glowing entranceway. There was no rush, no urgency, just a blissful sense of calm. I knew where I was going, and I was ecstatic.

But then I became aware of yet another presence in the tunnel, just ahead. And I knew it wasn't meant for me to get to the gates just yet.

You see, there was someone God wanted
me to meet.

CHAPTER THIRTEEN

After a week in the NICU, all we wanted to do was get to the Village. The Village was the part of the pediatric ICU where they moved the babies who were no longer critical but not quite strong enough to go home yet. One after another, we'd see a beaming set of parents say good-bye to the NICU nurses and skip happily over to the Village. Being there meant your baby didn't have to be in an incubator anymore — and that you could stay in the same room with them twenty-four hours a day. We longed to be the next ones to go, but it seemed we never were. The Village became our Promised Land.

The days turned into weeks, and the weeks into a month. Virgil had stopped going to work on the Air Force base so he could stay with us, but his sick days and leave days had almost run out. Once they did, we'd have no money coming in at all. I told Virgil he had to go home and get back to work, but he didn't want to leave me or the twins. And honestly, I didn't want him to leave us, either. We weren't out of the woods yet; no doctor ever told us our babies were definitely going to make it. Every time we seemed to turn a corner, some test result was bad or some monitor went off, and we were plunged right back into the horror of not knowing. One day the babies would surprise us by bottle-feeding, but then they'd quit and go back on feeding tubes. They also needed several blood transfusions starting right after they were born. It was a nonstop roller coaster of emotions. I didn't want Virgil to leave us, but I also didn't see any other choice. We were at the end of our rope.

That's when we learned Virgil's coworkers on the base had gotten together and donated their sick days and leave days to Virgil. He was going to be able to stay with me for at least three or four more weeks without missing a paycheck. That was incredible — just the thing we needed, just when we needed it. At the time, that seemed to me like a blessing born of the goodness of people — and of course it was — but there was more to it than that, much more. It's just that it took me a long time to see what that amazing gesture and the word "blessing" really meant.

And then, early one morning, after five weeks in the NICU, a nurse casually told us we were going to the Village.

We were finally *those* parents!

The nurse helped us give our babies their first baths in a little plastic hospital tub. Then we put their little preemie clothes on right over all their tubes and wires. *Come on, kids,* I thought, *we're getting outta here.*

Our room in the Village was small and simple — one crib, a twin bed, a recliner, and a bathroom — but to us it was a palace. We got to spend all night with the twins and hold them all day long. The first thing I noticed was that it was a lot noisier. The parents and nurses were more cheerful and chatty; plus, you could hear the occasional squeal of a crying baby — something you never heard in the NICU. One day, when I was in the hallway, I heard a baby's high-pitched cry, and I ran into our room to see if it was Willow or Micah. But it wasn't; it was the baby next door. I remember thinking how happy I'd be just to hear the twins cry or make any kind of noise at all. We were looking for a sign our babies had turned a corner — that they wanted to be here on this earth, with us, as much as we wanted to be here with them.

Then one day, we got that sign.

After a minute or two on the bottle, Willow pulled away, squinted her tiny eyes, looked up at me — and smiled.

Okay, it was a quick little smile, but it was definitely a smile — her very first one! Luckily, I had a camera with me, and I snapped a picture. I keep that photo in a special place, to remind me how important a simple smile can be.

A week passed, then another, then a third. The babies were ever-so-slowly improving, but there were still scary setbacks.

In our tenth week in the hospital, the twins were finally feeding on their own. The only remaining test they had to pass before they could be released was the car seat test. They had to prove they could sit in a car seat for however long it would take to get them home — which, in our case, was two hours. If they squirmed too much or seemed in distress, they'd flunk, and we'd be staying. At least I didn't have to worry about them having crying fits. Both the twins had started making little sounds, and when they got an immunization shot, they let out these adorable little half-cries/half-mews, like two kittens. I hated that they didn't like their shots, but I *loved* finally hearing them cry. Still, neither one was much of a wailer yet.

The day of the test arrived, and we helped strap Micah and Willow into their car seats. They were still way undersized, and the seat straps just swallowed them up. But, while Virgil and I watched and bit our nails, the babies passed the test with flying colors. The next day, a doctor came in and told us the good news.

"Congratulations, you're going home."

The day we left, both Micah and Willow weighed about 4.5 pounds.

We carefully put the twins in their car seats and strapped them into the back of the van. For the first few miles, Virgil probably drove twenty miles per hour. Honestly, it felt like we were driving with two big eggs in the back, and the slightest bump could crack them in half. Eventually, Virgil picked up speed — all the way up to 40 miles per hour. I'm pretty sure he never once got anywhere near the speed limit. Hey, we'd just spent ten weeks sweating out every little detail of our babies' existences, so we weren't about to start taking any chances now.

That's when *another* tornado hit.

Before driving back home, we stopped at Virgil's parents' home in Oklahoma City.

We wanted them to see the babies before we brought them home. While we were there, a nasty storm rolled in. Virgil and I debated spending the night with his parents, but it wasn't raining all that hard yet. We were really anxious to get home, so we hit the road, confident we'd beat the storm. But, like I said, in Oklahoma tornados can swoop in with almost no notice. We weren't on the road more than half an hour when the hard stuff came. Remember the terrible tornado that caused rain to fall on Willow's incubator? This one was even worse. The rain poured down in solid sheets, and the wind rocked our van back and forth. Suddenly we saw a bolt of lightning hit the ground two hundred yards away. It was so close, we felt the heat inside our van. I put my body over the two babies in case the windshield shattered. Another bolt of lightning hit, and I really started worrying we might not make it home in one piece.

It got so bad, Virgil finally had to pull off the road. We drove to Love's, a roadside country store and restaurant, and we sat in the car until the rain died down just enough for us to run inside. Mind you, both Micah and Willow were hooked up to baby monitors, these laptop-sized machines that alerted us if either of them stopped breathing. Not only did we have to run them inside, but once there, we had to quickly find a place to plug in their monitors. We charged through the front door, each carrying a baby — and ran into a wall of big, burly truckers.

"We have to plug in our babies!" Vigil yelled, pushing through. "We have to plug in our babies!"

We found a booth with an electrical socket nearby, and we settled in to ride out the storm. Many of the burly truckers came over to coo over the babies and talk to us about their own kids. It was another one of those lovely moments that blossomed in the midst of sheer chaos. When things are hard and miserable, I'd been learning all my life, there's an adventure in there somewhere waiting to happen.

Eventually, after the longest ten weeks and two-hour drive of our lives, we made it home. We spent the next few months making sure the twins stayed as healthy as possible. We even made people scrub up before they met the babies, and we gave everyone within a one-mile radius the third degree: Do you have a runny nose? Did you wash your hands? Was that a cough I just heard? When we pushed them around in their strollers, we covered them with a thin blanket to keep out contaminants, and when anyone tried to lift the blanket to get a quick peek, Virgil tugged it right back down. We must have looked like the weirdest parents, but, hey, we'd been through a lot. Virgil was trained in kung fu, and he kept saying he'd use it if he had to in order to keep germs away from our kids.

Slowly their personalities emerged. Micah had big, sad eyes and a constant expression of terror on his face. In photos where everyone else is smiling, he looks like he just saw a *T. rex.* He was the emotional one, the watcher, the worrier. Sweet as pie, but *so* serious. Willow, on the other hand, was calm and carefree. She just went about her business and giggled her way through life. One thing was clear: the twins were nuts for each other. Back in the NICU, the nurses bundled them together in the same blanket so they could feed together. They loved nuzzling each other, and one time Micah even started sucking on Willow's nose. They'd gone through hell together, and they'd pulled through together. Now they would forever be connected at the heart. Even in the womb their heartbeats were perfectly synched.

I'll never forget their first birthday and everything it meant, that we'd made it through the storm after all.

It should have been the happiest time of my life.

It should have been.

One night in my first year of marriage to Virgil, I woke up sometime after midnight and looked across the bed at my husband. He was lying there still and peaceful, but something was wrong. His chest and stomach were covered in blood, and so were our baby blue sheets. I looked down and saw I was covered in blood, too. I shot out of bed and screamed.

Virgil bolted awake. "What's wrong?" he asked. "What is it?" Then he looked down and saw the blood and touched it with his finger.

"Oh, sorry, babe," he said. "It's ice cream. I fell asleep eating ice cream."

I saw the half-empty bowl of chocolate ice cream by his side. We had a good laugh, and eventually my heart stopped racing. I guess my point in telling this story is that sometimes things aren't nearly as bad as they first seem. Sometimes the horrible stuff is just in your head.

In the months after my babies came home, I started feeling a great uneasiness in my life. Even though I had more stability than

I'd ever had before, I felt like everything was unsettled and out of whack. Don't get me wrong. I was so, so happy to be home with all my babies, and I was happy for a lot of other reasons, too. But, something was off. Something wasn't right.

It's painful for me to recall this period — because, again, it should have been the happiest time of my life — but the fact is, all those old feelings of anger and resentment were coming back. I felt a ton of stress and pressure, like everything that was wrong with my life was bubbling to the surface. I don't know why I suddenly felt this way — was it partly postpartum depression and partly just being tired of the struggle? Either way, I wasn't the easiest person to be around.

After the twins were born, Virgil's parents were extremely helpful, but along the way there were lots of little clashes. I couldn't escape the suspicion that Virgil's mom didn't think much of me as a mother. When the twins came, she was very helpful, but there were times when her comments struck me as criticisms. "Are you laying Willow on her back too much?" she'd say. I'd think, *Are you saying I don't hold my babies enough?* Virgil's mom is a kind and lovely woman and I'm sure she meant well, but I started feeling attacked. I didn't want anyone thinking I wasn't a good mother or a good wife. Virgil, of course, wound up taking the brunt of my feelings. I didn't blame him for anything that was happening, but he absorbed a lot of my anger and insecurity. And bit by bit, I pushed his family away.

Virgil's many great qualities as a father created another problem. I'd seen how he was willing to lose his job rather than leave our side in the hospital, and I knew how great and attentive he was with all the children. This made me realize, for the first time in my life, just how inattentive my own father had been. With my dad, his job always seemed to come first. And when the twins were born and teetered on the brink for all those weeks, my father didn't even bother to come down and see them. I felt like I had a score to settle with my father, and one night I sat down and wrote him a six-page e-mail listing all my grievances and telling him all about Virgil. "I want you to know what a real father looks like," I wrote.

I sent the e-mail and sat around the next day waiting for his reply. Finally, it came, and it was all of ten words.

"I can only imagine what you must think of me," is all he wrote.

I thought, *You don't have to imagine; I just*

told *you!*

But that was all he had to say. No apologies, no explanations. Looking back, I realize that was all he *could* say. He didn't have the language he needed to truly convey his feelings about anything. That's why he allowed me to beat him up over the phone and in my e-mail and all the times I was angry at him, without ever defending himself or saying a single bad word about my mom. He took it all, because he loved me. And that was the only way he knew how to show it — *by saying nothing.* But at the time, his lack of a reaction to my great unburdening only made me angrier.

And so I was done with my dad, too, and we stopped speaking.

Now, it wasn't like my first year with the twins was one bad thing after another, because it truly, truly wasn't. In fact, the more I started blocking out everyone else, the closer I pulled Virgil and the kids to me. And in that first year we had *so* much fun together as a family. Virgil was so happy with the twins, and I was thrilled to finally have my beautiful family. We laughed all the time, tickled by our great fortune. Most of the time I felt *incredibly* happy.

It's just that, underneath it all, I couldn't shake that feeling of unease. And suddenly I wasn't willing to be pushed around by anyone; I was determined to stand up against everyone I felt had wronged me. And so I started burning bridges left and right. I fought with Virgil — which we'd almost never done before — with his parents, with my parents, with everyone. All my life I'd desperately searched for a safe place I could call home, and now that I finally had one, I felt more lost and helpless than ever. Something was still missing — something big.

How could it be that I still felt so empty when I finally had the life I thought I wanted? Why couldn't I let go of the anger and the self-hatred that made me push away those who loved me most? Our lives can sometimes feel like a giant jigsaw puzzle, and we're always searching for those hard-to-find pieces that will make the puzzle come alive. But there is one piece that is key to making everything else fit, and if we don't find it, we'll forever be frustrated by what our puzzle is missing. "Whoever finds their life will lose it," it says in Matthew 10:39, "and whoever loses their life for My sake will find it."

The piece that I was missing was God.

And the greatest gift God gave me — the

gift that shook my soul and changed my life — was the gift of letting me see how much He loves me.

That first summer at home with my twins was when I began having those panic attacks. And just after they turned ten months was when I died.

THE CHILD

I moved with God and my angels through the tunnel, toward the glowing entranceway. I knew exactly where we were headed, and I believed I couldn't possibly feel any more joy than I did. But then I became aware of yet another presence in the tunnel, just ahead. This was the person God had brought me to meet.

This presence was smaller than my angels and also much more distinct. This figure had a body, and a face, and arms and legs.

It was a child.

It was a little girl.

I had the sensation of locking in on her and soaking up everything about her. She was small and no more than three or four years old. She had a white bonnet on her head, and she was holding a small white basket — sort of like a wicker Easter basket. She wore a white frilly summer dress that had tinges of yellow, and this yellow was the first identifiable color I saw in heaven. But it wasn't an ordinary yellow. These yellow tinges were beaming and sparkling like a prism, like they were reflecting the brilliant light around us and bouncing it back in an even more glorious way. The effect they created was just stunningly gorgeous, something I can't even think about now without losing my breath.

The girl was skipping and prancing and laughing, just like little kids do on Earth. She was bending and dipping her basket into the brightness at her feet and filling it up like she was filling it with water. She would dip the basket and scoop up the brightness and pour it out and do it again. And every time she dipped the basket and came up with it dripping this magical brightness, she laughed.

Every time she laughed, my spirit absolutely *swelled* with love and pride for her. I wanted to watch this little girl play for the rest of eternity. I wanted to run up to her and take her in my arms and tell her how much I loved her. The love just kept building, endless and radiating waves of love so deep and so intense and so unstopping I truly, truly believed my soul was going to explode and I was going to cease to exist. And all the while the little girl just kept dipping her basket and scooping up light and laughing like little girls do. It touched me so deeply, it was more than I could bear. I prepared myself to burst, to shatter into a million pieces, because I knew I couldn't possibly contain all the love I felt for this child.

And then God lifted this feeling from me.

It was almost as if I had been wearing some kind of magic glasses that suddenly He took off of me. And I knew it was God who lifted this feeling, because as soon as it was lifted, I looked back at the child and immediately understood who the child was.

The little girl with the golden basket was me.

And then another understanding passed between God and me, and I knew this is what He'd been trying to show me all my life. He'd been trying to show me how very much He loved me.

I knew God was allowing me to see myself *as He saw me.* And in His eyes I was an absolutely perfect creation, and I always would be. All the things that happened to me on Earth, all the bad decisions that caused me to hate myself — none of it mattered. I had believed God couldn't possibly love me, not after what had been done to me, not after what I had done. But this belief was a lie, and God blasted the lie by showing me the intensity of His love for me.

Seeing the child was the most profound and powerful thing that ever happened to me, because it did something I didn't think was possible.

It made me whole.

In that moment, chains that had bound me all my life fell away. Chains of shame and secrets and lies and pain. Chains too heavy for anyone or anything to free me from on

Earth. Chains that simply dropped away in the presence of the truth.

This was the key sensation — that the truth of all truths had been revealed to me. I was imbued with this penetrating understanding that God had always loved me, like He loves all His children. And so, for the first time ever, I was filled with love for myself. How could I not love myself? I was God's perfect creation!

What's more, God chose to show me myself at the age of three. This was not a random age. I was three years old when the abuse began. That was the turning point in my life, the point where my innocence was taken from me. Though I had many happy times as a child and many moments of love and goodness, the truth is that from the age of three on I was trapped in a life of shame and secrets, of self-doubt and self-hatred — of believing I didn't deserve God's love, of believing God had abandoned me.

So God took me back to when I was three years old, and He *freed* me from that lie. All those dark and difficult years, every crisis and heartbreak that made me turn away from Him — all of it, every bit of it, was washed clean by the awareness that God's love for me is boundless. Burdens I had been shouldering for decades were lifted. Seeing myself through God's eyes made me whole and set me free.

Yet even as I was filled with God's love, I knew I was experiencing only a tiny, minuscule *grain* of it. God's love is so big and so vast and so powerful, we can only contain a small part. That tiny grain of God's love filled me so completely that I couldn't imagine being anywhere else but with Him.

Then I heard something in a way I hadn't heard anything else in heaven. It wasn't like the pure communication that had passed between God and me. It was a word, spoken by a voice.

"Crystal."

It was my mother's voice. She was calling my name. The sound was so sharp and so abrupt that I knew she was screaming.

"Crystal! *Crystal!*"

For the first time I had the sensation of stopping — like the feeling of seeing a car coming at you and freezing in your tracks. And in that instant I realized my mother didn't know where I was. She didn't know I was okay. I felt sorry for what she had to be going through. The truth is, I hadn't thought at all about my hospital room. I didn't hover above my bed or see everyone clustered around me or anything like that. I had no connection to anything that was happening in that room or on Earth. Even the vision of my children wasn't earthly; it was an awareness, like everything else I was experiencing in heaven. But that all changed when I heard my mother yell my name. All of a sudden I knew I had to let her know where I was.

"I need to tell my mother I'm okay," I said.

And God responded. *"The choice is up to you."*

I didn't want to leave God. I didn't want to go anywhere. I just wanted to let my mother know I was okay. I had the sensation of turning around and, for the first time, focusing on what was beneath me. It was a floor of what looked like shimmering water crystals, shining like a billion perfect diamonds. I could not see through it, but I knew that my mother's voice was coming from somewhere beneath it. As I turned away from the entrance to heaven, there was another communication from God — the last and most powerful thing He said to me.

"Tell them what you can remember."

"I'm going to remember everything," I answered. "I will be right back."

I focused my full attention on the water crystals again, and in that instant I knew I was back in my human body.

And that's when I opened my eyes.

CHAPTER FOURTEEN

The first thing I saw was a nurse's face. It was right over me, only a few inches away. Her mouth was moving — she was yelling.

"Do you know where you are? Do you know what day it is?"

I looked to my left and I saw my mother, her face wet with tears.

"Crystal!" the nurse screamed. "Do you know where you are? Tell me where you are."

I heard her questions clearly, but I didn't answer right away. It was almost like talking was something foreign to me. I had just come from a place where there was no need to talk. I tried to speak, but nothing came out. The yelling continued. I tried again. Finally, I found the words.

"I am in the most beautiful light," I mumbled. "I am with God."

And then I closed my eyes, so I could

make my way back to heaven.

The nurse yelled again.

"Crystal, I need you to look at me! What are your children's names?"

I opened my eyes, and I tried to say my kids' names. I said the names of Payne and Sabyre but couldn't come up with Willow and Micah, and that really frustrated me. And anyway it wasn't what I wanted to talk about.

I turned to my mother this time, and I said, "It's okay. I'm in the most beautiful light. I am with God."

"I know, I know," my mother said, "but I need you to get back here with me."

But I had no intention of staying. I closed my eyes again and tried to go back, but for some reason I couldn't. It was like there was a blockage. I felt like all these people yelling at me were literally separating my spirit from heaven. I was frustrated. The nurses kept asking me questions, and I tried to answer them quickly so I could get back to heaven. I kept trying and trying to go, but I just couldn't.

And then I heard a man's voice. I opened my eyes and saw a doctor holding a syringe.

"Crystal, I'm going to give you a shot," he said. "On a pain scale of one to ten, this is going to be a ten."

He leaned in and poked the needle into my arm. Instantly I felt my jaw clamp down and every muscle in my body clench tight. The pain followed after that. It was a great, surging pain that swept through my body, building and building and consuming me. It was almost like I could *hear* the pain — like a gigantic freight train rumbling through my body, getting closer, going faster, intensifying, tearing me apart.

"It's almost over," I heard the doctor say.

What was happening to me? Why was I trapped this way? *"Once we get there, you cannot come back,"* God had communicated to me, and I understood Him . . . but I hadn't passed through the gates yet, so why couldn't I go back? *"The choice is up to you,"* He had said. The choice had been mine! As the pain tore through me, I closed my eyes tightly, and I tried desperately to escape and to somehow, somehow, make my way to heaven.

But by then I think I already knew I wasn't going back.

CHAPTER FIFTEEN

We live pretty much in the middle of the United States, where the Great Plains meet the Bible Belt. We're only a few hours south of the exact geographic center of the country in Kansas. The land where we are in Oklahoma is broad and flat and beautiful. We're surrounded by thousands of acres of raw and rugged prairies, most of which probably look the same today as they did back when it all began. In the Wichita Mountains Wildlife Refuge, where we like to take the kids when we can, you can see so many of God's great creatures — elk and longhorns, black-tailed prairie dogs and white-tailed deer, mallards and hawks and lizards, and of course the proud buffalo. The Native American poet N. Scott Momaday said that when you gaze out on this ancient land, "your imagination comes to life. And this, you think, is where creation was begun."

There is so much beauty on this earth,

and in every bird and blade of grass we can see the hand of God. I know how lucky we are to be here, among His many gifts. But even so, there came a time when I forgot to be thankful for the amazing blessing of being here.

You see, I'd been to a place even more beautiful, and all I wanted to do was go back.

All in all, I stopped breathing on my own for nine minutes. There were two minutes between when my face turned blue and when the first nurse rushed into my room, and another seven minutes during which doctors worked to revive me after my lungs shut down. I went into full respiratory arrest, and if my mother hadn't been in the room with me when it happened, I'm pretty sure you wouldn't be reading these words.

Why did it happen? It's one of those things where no one can say for sure. The most likely explanation is that my pain pump wasn't set up properly, which meant I was receiving more of the painkiller Dilaudid than my body could handle. What painkillers do is basically block the receptors in your brain that signal your body that you're in pain. But too much medicine can shut down the receptors altogether, and your brain stops telling your lungs to function. And if your lungs stop getting oxygen to your heart and your heart stops pumping blood to your brain, all your organs quit.

Did I actually die? That's also hard to say. I couldn't breathe, and I had no pulse. And certainly if no nurses and doctors had rushed in when they did, I would have died sometime during those nine minutes. But you aren't considered clinically dead until a doctor officially calls your time of death, which usually happens five minutes after they stop trying to revive you. Some people say that when your heart stops beating and your lungs shut down, you're basically dead, but as long as your brain is still functioning, there's a chance you can be pulled back from the brink. That's what happened to me. The doctors blasted my lungs with oxygen and got me breathing on my own before my brain, and I, were dead.

Still, I always tell people that I died and came back. I'm not a doctor and I don't know if technically that is 100 percent right, but I do know I was no longer in my human body. I know without any doubt that I passed on to another world. And, hey, it's easier to say I died than start explaining patient-controlled analgesia and brain receptors.

All things considered, my mother had a harder time in those nine minutes than I did. I was no longer in that hospital room, but she was stuck there watching her daughter turn ten shades of blue. My mom remembers one doctor climbing on top of me and pounding my chest, and she remembers all the doctors working so hard that they were sweating straight through their scrubs. It must have been terrifying. At first she stayed away from my bed and prayed quietly in the back of the room, but after a few desperate minutes she said, "This is all in Your hands now, God," and found a spot where she could touch my hair and tell me she loved me. "Please, Crystal, stay with us; don't go," she begged me over and over. "If you can, please come back. *Please come back.*"

My mother always says my nine minutes in heaven were her nine minutes in hell.

The first good sign for my mom was when she heard a doctor say, "Her eyes fluttered." That's when she started yelling my name. As soon as the doctors saw I was back in my body, they sprang into action. They gave me a shot of Narcan, which is used to counter the effects of an overdose. It basically blocks any narcotics from reaching your receptors so that your lungs and heart get the signals to start working again.

But it also frees up the receptors to start sending pain signals again, which is why my body was instantly racked with unbelievable pain. And once *that* pain subsided, I started to feel the really sharp pain of my pancreatitis again. They moved me to the intensive care unit and eventually put me back on painkillers, and I spent the next few days slipping in and out of a deep, medicated sleep. I was so out of it the nurses had to wake me up and force me to eat Jell-O; I lost something like fifteen pounds in ten days. I only vaguely remember everyone coming to see me — Virgil and my mother, of course; and Virgil's parents; and JP and Sabyre; and my brother, Jayson; and even my father, who came down from Illinois. All of the people I had pushed away were the first ones by my side. But I was so groggy I don't remember much about those visits at all.

What I do remember clearly — and what lingered for a long time — was how I felt about being back in my human form. To put it mildly, I was pretty ticked off. I simply loved being with God so much and wanted to go back so badly that I came to resent all the people who saved my life. The doctors, the nurses, my mother, even Virgil — anyone who *wanted* me to come back had, in my mind, prevented me from returning to heaven. "Why did you make me come back?" I asked them over and over in those first few hours. "This was not my choice."

Now, some of you may say, "Hold on a minute, weren't you thrilled to be back with your husband and your children?" Some of you may even wonder, *How could you choose to stay in heaven when you knew your family would be so crushed to lose you?* Those are good questions, and I've thought about them a lot in the last three years. And the answer I come up with is always the same: more than anything, I wanted to be with God.

Believe me, before this happened I could not understand how it was possible to love anyone or anything more than your own children. But that was before I found myself in the presence of God. Like I said, that changed everything. I understood instantly that the love of God is greater and more powerful than any other kind of love. And I didn't only understand it; I *felt* it and heard it and saw it and tasted it with every fiber of my being. When I was in my spirit form, there was simply no other conceivable option for me but to be with God. I know it sounds funny to say, but not even my babies made me want to return to my human form. I've discussed this with my children, and, honestly, I think it hurts their feelings a bit. Once in a while they like to tease me about it, sort of how they tease me about being late to pick them up at school. "Gee, thanks a lot, Mom," they'll say. "Thanks for choosing us."

But in my first days back from heaven, that's just how I felt. Even though I'd been blocked from returning, I still felt incredibly infused by God and by the whole miraculous experience. I still felt far more connected to my spirit form than to my human form. But beyond that, I just really, really *missed* God. I longed to be with Him again, and I felt like I was still bathed in the glow of His greatness. When Moses came down from Mount Sinai after speaking with God, his face glowed so brightly, he had to cover it with a cloth so the people wouldn't be afraid of him. That is something like what I was feeling inside. I mean, it wasn't like I had met the president or a celebrity or something. This was the Creator of the universe! The Lord God of Israel!

That is not something you can just shake off.

Gradually, over the course of a few days, I did begin to feel grateful I was with my family again. They all rushed to be with me, even the ones I had tried so hard to push away. I still missed God, but being around my loved ones made me realize again that life is a wonderful gift to be cherished and treasured. It wasn't like a switch being flipped where suddenly I was thrilled to be back. It happened over time, as I got my human legs back and began to see glimpses of God's guiding hand here on Earth. For instance, just a day after I was discharged from the hospital we celebrated Sabyre's birthday in our home. We had a lot of friends over, and we served ice cream and opened presents. I sat with my tiny twins in my arms, first one and then the other, and right there in my living room I felt grateful to be back with my family again. I felt blessed to have such beautiful children and such a wonderful husband. For the first time since coming back, I felt happy.

Then, one week later, it was Christmas. My brother asked if we could come up to Oklahoma City and spend the holiday with him, so we bundled up the kids and hit the road. We put all the wrapped Christmas presents in the back of the van beneath a blanket, so the twins wouldn't see them and start asking us about Santa Claus. It was smooth driving for maybe five minutes before another one of those nasty Oklahoma storms rolled in. Freezing wind, sheets of ice and snow. Virgil could barely see five feet in front of him, so we couldn't drive much faster than ten or fifteen miles per hour, and even that felt treacherous. We noticed huge snowdrifts building up alongside the highway, and we pulled over in a nearby town to figure out if we should keep going. But the bad weather was in front of us *and* behind us, so we had nowhere to escape to. We decided to keep moving forward as carefully as we could.

The two-hour trip wound up taking thirteen hours. The windshield wipers kept freezing and getting stuck, and Virgil had to hop out and fix them. We kept passing people who spun out or were stuck in a snowbank, and Virgil would stop and give them a push so they could get back on the road. We couldn't see any highway signs because of the dense snow, so after a while we didn't even know where we were. We were terrified a stretch of highway would be shut down, stranding us in the middle of nowhere, but, luckily, the roads stayed open. After a few hours the kids were starving, so I broke into the picnic basket of sausage and cheese and crackers I'd packed. A few hours later, when that was all gone, we ate the candies and chocolates out of our Christmas stockings.

At one point we got stuck ourselves, near a parking lot in Oklahoma City. Cars were stalled out everywhere, and other cars were skidding on ice and crashing into them. It took us two hours to dig our way out of the snow, but with the help of some other drivers, Virgil wedged boards under the tires and managed to move the van. Then we got stuck *again* just a few blocks from my brother's house. I was so scared and so tired at that point that I just wanted to grab the four kids and start walking. Fortunately, three men appeared out of nowhere and helped Virgil dig out the van again. We eventually made it to my brother's home in one piece.

It had been a really trying thirteen hours, and there were times when I was really afraid something bad was going to happen. But the fact is, we were all warm and cozy in the van, we had plenty of food, and the kids had a blast eating their Christmas chocolates. For much of those thirteen hours we actually had *fun.* The highways stayed open, we didn't run out of gas, and we made it to my brother's house safe and sound. Perhaps most striking of all, I got to see the very best of the human spirit at work. I watched Virgil selflessly get out of our warm van time and time again to help people dig their cars out of snow, and I watched total strangers come over and help us when we needed them most. I felt deeply moved by the incredible acts of kindness I had witnessed.

And when that realization struck me, I felt truly happy to be back here on Earth. Remember I described Oklahoma's great plains and rugged mountains and beautiful wildlife and all its many gifts from God? Well, I forgot a big one — Oklahoma's people. That dark night on the dangerous highway, I saw the hand of God at work again, this time in his human creations. And that touched my heart and stirred my soul and made me feel blessed once again to be here among His many wonderful gifts.

After I got past being upset with everyone I felt had dragged me back from heaven, I realized all the grudges and grievances that had cluttered my soul for so long had disappeared. It was like God wiped the slate completely clean. And the big stuff — the resentments I'd lived with for so many years — just melted away. I'd been angry with someone who owed Virgil money — and I'm talking a lot of money, not just a few hundred bucks, but a life-changing amount. But afterward I told him, "I know we're never getting that money back, and it's okay. We have to pray for them." Virgil looked at me funny, because he knew I didn't part with money easily. He says that's when he truly believed I'd been with God — when I was okay with writing off a debt. But that just showed the magnitude of the forgiveness God washed over me.

I don't know. I just felt liberated from all the baggage I'd carried my whole life. I asked Virgil's mother to forgive me for pushing her away. I asked Virgil to forgive me for making him choose between his family and me. I asked my brother to forgive me for not paying enough attention to him when we were young, and I asked my mother to forgive me for always making her the target of my anger. I even called my father in Illinois, and I asked him to forgive me, too.

"Oh no, you don't need to apologize for anything," he said.

"But I do," I told him. "I need you to forgive me for being so hard on you."

I also stopped being so attached to my possessions. I'd always been very sentimental about objects that meant something to me, but after I died I no longer cared much about material things. I told my friends, "If you ever liked anything in my house, this'd be a good time to ask for it, because I'm ready to give it all away." Honestly, I wouldn't have cared if we *did* give everything away and moved into a one-room shack. After I died I came to realize that my fortune was my family and friends and the love of God, and the rest didn't matter all that much.

I found I loved and cared about *everyone.* People I'd been furious at — like JP's dad and Sabyre's dad — I suddenly felt deep love and compassion for. I was filled with sorrow and pity for anyone who had ever wronged or hurt me, and I prayed for them because they were God's perfect creations. I knew that just as that happy little girl in the light had been hurt badly in her lifetime, so, too, had those who had hurt me. They, too, were once innocent children, and that's how God still saw them — as children He loved no matter what. Knowing what I knew, I didn't want a single person in the world, not even my worst enemy, to stand outside God's radiance — I wanted everyone to be there with me in the glory of His greatness. I'd held my share of grievances, and I'd been a judgmental person. On occasion after I died I'd catch myself judging someone again, but I'd quickly tell myself, *No, Crystal. Remember what He did for you.* And the judgment would just go away.

My disappointment at leaving God's side eventually lessened, but this elation and joy I felt at having been in His presence never did — it only got stronger. Nothing bothered me or made me angry anymore, and I overflowed with compassion and love. I had been powerfully transformed by those nine minutes, and in every way that mattered I was a new creation.

After a lifetime of doubt I was a loving child of God, and nothing would ever be the same again.

I realize now that I began telling my story just a second or two after I returned. "I am in the most beautiful light," I had told the nurse, and then I told the same thing to my mother. My mom says no sooner had I come back from heaven than I told the doctor who revived me I had been with God, and she remembers the doctor hearing those words and beginning to cry. He was a man of faith and believed I had been to heaven, so he wept with joy.

I was drugged up pretty heavily the next few days, but once I felt better I found I couldn't wait to talk about what happened.

I wanted to tell everyone where I'd been and what I'd seen. Naturally, I told Virgil the whole story, and he was moved to tears. I told my mother, and I told every doctor and nurse who wandered anywhere near my room. Finally, when they moved me out of the ICU and into a regular room, I got the chance to tell someone who was not a relative or a doctor or nurse.

I was alone one evening when an elderly cleaning woman walked into my room. She was mopping the floor and humming some old gospel song. I was still in a lot of pain, but I turned my neck as much as I could to look at her and cleared my throat.

"Do you believe in God?" I asked her.

"Oh yes, honey," the cleaning woman said.

"I just died and saw God," I said. "I was in His presence."

The woman kept mopping and said, "Yes, child, praise to God."

I was surprised by how nonchalant she was, and I asked her if she believed me.

"Oh yes, child, I believe. Oh yes, I believe."

And then she went right back to mopping and humming her song.

It wasn't that she didn't feel my time in heaven was a miracle. It's just that she had believed in God's greatness for most of her life, and I'd only been sure of it for a handful of days. Her faith was so great, she wasn't the least bit surprised by what God had done for me. And I found that to be *incredible.* My spirit was lifted by the strength of her belief, and I couldn't wait to tell more people about what had happened to me.

Eight days after I died I was finally released from the hospital. Although my pancreatitis was gone, my body was still really sore. I felt like I had a whole rack of cracked ribs. Just to dull the pain, I had to hold a pillow against my stomach any time I coughed or laughed.

A couple of days after I came home I got a call from a bill collector. I interrupted him in the middle of him telling me about my overdue account.

"Do you believe in God?" I asked.

"Um, yes," he said.

I launched into my story of dying and going to heaven and standing with God. When I was done, there was a long pause before he spoke again.

"So," he said, "can we expect your payment this week?"

Everywhere I went, I looked for opportunities to tell my story. One time, Virgil and I were in a meeting with four or five other

Christians we knew. I had already told someone there my story, and they asked me to share it with the group. I've never been comfortable speaking in public, but there weren't that many people at the meeting. So I took a deep breath and got right to it. When I was done, I expected someone to ask me for more details about my time with God. I assumed they'd want to know everything. But not a single person in the room asked me a question. There was just silence and a few thank-yous, and then we moved on to another topic. And in that moment a terrible thought popped into my head: *They think I'm lying! Or they think I'm crazy!*

For the first time, I felt stupid for telling my story. It had never occurred to me that anyone wouldn't believe what I was saying, and I'd assumed everyone would be as excited about it as I was. But the people in that meeting either didn't believe me or didn't care. That was a shocking realization. My face turned beet red, and I sat there feeling utterly embarrassed and mortified. I wanted to jump up and say, *"You're all missing the point. Don't you know why we're here?"* I could feel myself withdrawing deeper and deeper into my shell.

Still, I couldn't contain my urge to share what happened with the world, so I picked my times and I kept telling my story. I truly wanted to express the passion I was feeling for God. But more often than not, the reaction I got was not what I expected. Sure, some people seemed genuinely moved, but others just kind of listened and smiled and moved on with their lives. I got another chance to share my story with a small group, which included one person who'd heard me tell it before. When I finished, this person looked at me and said, "Gosh, you talk about that a lot." I was stunned. It wasn't like I was telling them how I'd met a celebrity or the president. I was talking about being with God! Why weren't these people as moved and overjoyed as I was? What was I doing wrong?

The last straw came about three weeks after my release from the hospital. I was with a group of people in an informal setting, and the discussion turned to God. I started telling someone what I had experienced and how wonderful it had been to be with God. Nearby I noticed a woman roll her eyes — you know, that look that says, "Oh no, here she goes again." I immediately stopped talking and left the room. I felt stupid and embarrassed, and worst of all I felt like no one believed me. I decided then and there I wouldn't tell another soul about what happened. I was going to go back to teaching soon, and the last thing I needed was for the town to start buzzing about how crazy I was. I just shut down.

It was that moment when I became totally human again.

For the next few months I cried at night, because I missed God so much and because I could no longer share my story. *"Tell them what you can remember,"* God had said, but when I tried to do that I just wound up looking and feeling foolish. I still didn't have the answer to the one burning question I had left: Why did God send me back? If He wanted me to tell everyone about His glory, why was He making it so no one believed me? I still had the strong desire to talk about Him nonstop, but I also felt that everywhere I turned, doors were shutting on me. I didn't know what to do anymore.

But during this trying time there was one person who listened to my story. Every night Virgil would turn to me in bed and say, "Tell me about it again. Tell me everything that happened again." Not once in a while — *every single night.* And so I'd face Virgil and wipe away my tears, and I'd say, "Well, I closed my eyes and went to sleep, and then I remember waking up in heaven." Virgil would hang on my every word, and together we would praise God.

And Virgil might have been the last person to ever hear my story, if something remarkable hadn't happened a few months later in, of all places, our kitchen.

CHAPTER SIXTEEN

It's kind of ironic I was so upset by people not believing me. I mean, I was the world's biggest skeptic until all this happened. If someone had come up to me a few years ago and told me they died and went to heaven, I'm pretty sure I would have smiled politely and walked away thinking they were nuts. The truth is, if someone came up to me *today* and told me they had stood with God, I can't say I would automatically believe them. I understand that a story like this isn't the easiest thing to swallow. Not everyone can feel as certain about God's great power as that wonderful cleaning woman.

The reaction I got to my story — and that one eye roll in particular — made me step back and think harder about what had happened. I certainly didn't think I was crazy, but the fact that some people *did* caused a little doubt to creep into my mind. Was I remembering things correctly? Was it possible my brain had played a trick on me? There are all kinds of theories about why people report having visions — or what doctors call episodic experiences — when they hover close to death. When a person stops breathing, they can have tunnel vision, which could explain the tunnel so many people see. When your heart stops beating, you can see bright lights, which some people say is a medical phenomenon, not a spiritual one. And when your brain loses oxygen, it can start firing neurons that haven't been fired in years or even decades, which can trigger memories of long-ago people and experiences. Hard-core skeptics can find a way to dismiss any story about heaven as nothing more than a medical hiccup.

Then again, all those experts are basing their opinions on medical books, not first-hand knowledge. How can they say something is real or not real if they've never experienced it themselves? And how do you explain the presence of God in these "episodic experiences"? It's one thing to see a relative who has passed on, but what kind of neuron produces the powerful radiance I immediately recognized as God? How do you explain the feeling of absolutely bursting with God's love? In the months after it

287

happened, I spent countless hours sitting and thinking about those fateful nine minutes. I needed to be sure about what, exactly, had happened to me.

One of the first things I realized is that I forgot a lot more about the experience than I remembered. I've described the very clear feeling I had that there were open channels between me and my angels and God, and that we were able to pass unlimited and instant information back and forth. Most important, those channels allowed me to fully understand the perfection of God's plan. God allowed me to see the absolute truth about everything that matters in life. Before I could even ask the questions, God gave me all the answers.

But then, when I returned to my human form, I no longer had those answers. I still understood that God's plan is perfect, but I didn't know what that plan was or why it was perfect. Try as I might, I couldn't remember what had passed between my angels and me, though I knew we exchanged *mountains* of insight in a constant, free-flowing, wordless, beautiful conversation. It was like that dream I had about God's plan, the one that prompted me to wake Virgil so I could describe it to him. The next morning, I'd forgotten all the key details, though my memory of the dream itself was still very powerful. That is what my time in heaven felt like — I could easily summon the overall miracle and majesty of it, but I couldn't recall a lot of what filled me with such joy when I was there.

Perhaps we're not meant to have that kind of infinite understanding here on Earth. If we were, we wouldn't need to have faith, because we'd be so sure about everything. There's a reason we can't have that knowledge now, and God knows that reason. All we can do is have faith in God and in His plan for us. The incredible gift God gave me is the certainty that His plan is perfect.

What I do recall most clearly is God's final directive to me: *"Tell them what you can remember."* He didn't say to tell them what happened; He said to tell them what I could *remember.* Maybe it's just beyond human ability to describe or even understand the full glory of heaven with the tools we have on Earth. " 'What no eye has seen, what no ear has heard, and what no human mind has conceived' — the things God has prepared for those who love him," it says in 1 Corinthians 2:9. But God knows that remembering even a small fraction of what He showed me was more than powerful enough to completely change my life. It's like how even a tiny glimpse of God's love filled me up so much I just about burst. Maybe we can't handle more than a sliver of God's reality. But since His plan is perfect, I know a sliver is all we need.

And so I did what God told me to do, and I shared everything I could remember. And that's what I've shared with you in this book, nothing more or less. Like I said, if I were going to make up a story, it would've been much more dramatic than mine is. And, if I wanted to make it really powerful, I would have said I met my second child — the child I lost when I had an abortion.

Many people who hear my story assume the little girl I saw — the girl who dipped her basket in the light — was the child I lost. It made sense to them that God was giving me the chance to meet the daughter I never knew. But that thought didn't occur to me. I knew as soon as God lifted the feeling of overwhelming love that the girl was me.

When I told my mother about the little girl, she began to cry. When she got home later, she dug through her closets and pulled out some old family albums. After a while, she found what she was looking for — a faded color photograph of me as a little girl. In the picture, I'm wearing a white bonnet on my head and a white summer dress tinged with yellow. I'm not holding an Easter basket, but my mom got me one of those, too. She remembers how I loved taking it everywhere.

In the photo I am three years old.

I don't remember that photo or the dress or the basket, but I'm not surprised my mother found it. And I will never have the slightest doubt why God showed that precious little girl to me.

Yet, as sure as I was of what I had seen and what it meant, I was a lot less sure about sharing my story with anyone. I didn't know if I could handle another eye roll or another look of indifference. Inside, I yearned to talk about God, but doing it in public made me feel like an idiot. So I shut down and didn't tell anyone for several long months. The greatest thing that ever happened to me got packed away in mothballs.

Until, out of the blue, a woman I knew named Pauline called me in July 2010, seven months after I died. That phone call was the start of something truly miraculous.

"Crystal, will you come share your testimony with a few people I go to church with?"

At the time I was running a small day care

out of our home, and Pauline was the director of the food program that helped us with our meals for the kids. I'd told her my story way back in January, and now here she was, months later, calling to ask me to tell it to her friends. It took me about two seconds to answer.

"I'd really rather not," I said.

Pauline wasn't having it. She said it was a group of only four or five people. She'd already told them about me, and they were anxious to hear my testimony. I hemmed and hawed, but Pauline was insistent. Sometime during our conversation it occurred to me that Pauline's church was in Thomas, a small town two hours north of me. If I did tell my story there, at least I wouldn't know anyone and would never have to see them again.

But so far I'd shared my story only in casual settings, and this would be more like giving a speech. I absolutely *hate* speaking in public. My face gets blotchy, and I get the sweats whenever I have to get up and talk to more than a few people at a time. Still, I'd been secretly itching to talk about God again to someone other than Virgil. And it was only a handful of people in a tiny town two hours away. What was the worst that could happen? A few facial blotches? Pauline eventually wore me down, and I agreed to give the talk.

As soon as I agreed, I regretted it, but I figured I could always back out if the pressure got too bad.

A few days later Pauline called and told me she was sending me a flyer she'd made about my talk. A flyer? Why would she need a flyer for five people? Two days after that she called and asked if I'd mind if she invited a couple more people. I got the feeling Pauline had bamboozled me.

"You know, I really don't think I can do this," I told her.

"Oh, sure you can," she said.

In the weeks before my talk I started to lose a lot of sleep. I was on the verge of calling Pauline to cancel the whole thing when, with just two weeks to go, I was in my kitchen cooking dinner, standing over the stove, stirring and tasting, adding this and that, hoping whatever it was came out okay. I'm not a very good cook, if you must know, and that bothers me more than it probably should. Virgil was by the sink washing sippy cups. We were chatting about our day and our kids and what groceries we needed. It was a normal evening, or as normal as my life had been ever since I died ten months earlier.

Then, all of a sudden, it happened. The message, the nudge — I call it different things. The best way I can describe the feeling that suddenly overcame me is to say I felt like I had God all over me. I felt *infused* by God, head to toe. It wasn't as intense as the feeling of bathing in His love in heaven — but then that happened to me when I was in my spirit form. This was happening in my kitchen! I'd felt these little nudges from God before — like when He told me to tip the waitress $100 — but this one was particularly strong and clear. It was five simple words suddenly thrust into my being.

Tell them the whole story.

I dropped my spoon and jumped back from the stove. I buried my face in my hands and cried, "Oh, God . . . oh, God." Virgil rushed to my side.

"Are you okay? Did you burn yourself?"

"He wants me to tell them everything," I blurted out. "He wants me to tell them *everything*!"

Virgil knew immediately who "He" was. And we both knew what "everything" meant. God didn't want me to just talk about my time in heaven. He wanted me to talk about my *life,* too. He wanted me to share my deepest secrets — the very things

I'd spent a lifetime trying to hide. The sexual abuse, the self-loathing, the abortion — everything.

"Why is He doing this?" I kept asking. "Oh, God, please don't make me do this."

Virgil, as he usually does in moments when I lose my cool, didn't say much; he just held me and comforted me. In all those months of listening to my heaven story night after night, he never once acted like he was tired of hearing it. He never once said, "Crystal, this is getting a little old." The strength of his faith was a huge comfort to me, and his incredible love for God always picked me up when I needed it most. And with me standing there crying my eyes out and questioning God, Virgil knew I needed it now more than ever.

"If this is something you feel you can't do, then pray and ask God to take it away from you," he said calmly. "But if He doesn't, then be obedient and do what He wants you to do."

How could I argue with that?

For the next two weeks I prayed and cried about it every night. I asked God over and over, "Please, don't make me do this," and I waited for one of His infusions that would lift the burden from me. But there was no infusion, no message, no nudge. Before I knew it, it was the night before my speech in Thomas. *God,* I thought, *if You're going to lift this, You better do it now. You're seriously running out of time.* I clung hard to the hope that He would let me back out at the last minute, but just in case, I knew there was something I needed to do before my talk.

I needed to tell my mother about my abortion.

Nearly fifteen years had passed since it had happened, and I'd managed to keep it a secret from my mother all that time. If it had been up to me, I never would have told her. God had freed me from my shame, but still I didn't want to cause my family any pain. And now God wanted me to take this thing I'd buried deeply in my past and share it with the world. If I was going to do that, I owed it to my mother to tell her first. I was absolutely *dreading* that conversation, but I knew I had to do it.

The night before my speech, I picked up the phone and called my mom. When she answered, I was already blubbering.

"What's wrong, sweetheart?" she said. "Tell me what's wrong."

I tried to talk, but I couldn't stop crying. Getting the words out was so much harder than I'd expected, and I'd expected it to be *really* hard. "Mom, I have to tell you something," I blurted out between sniffles. "But you're going to be so ashamed of me."

"It's okay, baby," my mom said. "Just spit it out."

It felt like an hour before I finally muttered the truth. There was silence on her end, and I knew her heart was breaking. I waited for the "How could you?" and the "What were you thinking?" I waited for her judgment.

Instead, my mom told me she loved me and didn't think any less of me. She said she was sorry I had to go through it alone, and she wished I'd gotten better advice before I did it.

"I'm sorry you didn't come to me," she said sadly. "I'm sorry I wasn't able to be there for you."

It was one of the hardest conversations I've ever had in my life. But once it was over, I was surprised by how relieved I felt. A dark secret I'd harbored for so many years was — just like that — not a secret anymore. God kept lifting the curtain of shame I'd drawn around myself.

The next morning, a warm October Saturday, Virgil and I packed up the kids and set out for Thomas, Oklahoma.

I hadn't told my children about my abuse

or abortion, so our plan was for Virgil to stay with all four kids in the church's playground while I gave my speech inside. When I was young, my mom shared way too many things with me — adult stuff I shouldn't have had to worry about — and I didn't want to be that way with my kids. I wanted to shield them from things they didn't need to know yet. After my speech, we planned to go to a pumpkin patch that had a corn maze and a hayride, and JP and Sabyre were excited about that. They had no idea their mom was on the verge of totally losing it.

I don't think I slept a wink that night, but I was too nervous to feel tired. On the whole ride up I just prayed and prayed for God to take this away from me. I was wearing capri pants and a nice shirt, something casual, but honestly I don't even remember dressing myself that morning. It was almost like I was in a trance.

And then, when we got to the church in Thomas, I saw it wasn't just four or five women milling around; it was more like *thirty* women!

I was horrified. I went straight to the church nursery with my twins and hid out there. I didn't want to see or talk to anyone. After a while the group served brunch, but

I was way too anxious to eat. I sat at a back table with Virgil and the kids and I tried to avoid all eye contact. The good ol' Crystal Shut Down was in full effect.

Finally, when brunch was finished, it was time for my speech. My heart was beating so hard it was like a sledgehammer pounding in my chest. Virgil took the kids out back, where they had this big wooden Noah's Ark for them to play in. I wished so much I could climb into that big ark and hide out with them. I went into the church sanctuary and took my seat in the very back pew and kept praying to God.

They had a small stage with a drum set and guitar, and someone played a few songs to get things started. Every time they began a new song I was so happy, because that gave me another four or five minutes to pray. I still hadn't given up hope that God would take this burden from me, which meant all I'd have to do is get up and talk about His glory. The thought of talking about my abortion to a roomful of strangers was making me physically ill.

When the last song ended, I saw Pauline make her way to the podium. She thanked everyone for coming and said a few words about God. Then she started talking about me. My heart was beating louder than the drums. She told everyone how I'd gotten sick in December, and how I died and came back, and how I had shared my story with her, and that was why I was there. And then she looked at me and said, "Crystal, come on up."

I don't know how my knees didn't give out, but somehow I made it to the podium. On the way there I kept praying and praying. God still had time to take this away. But, seriously, He'd be cutting it *really* close. *God, if You're not going to take this from me,* I pleaded, *at least stand beside me.*

I looked out at the roomful of women, and I immediately felt my face break out in red blotches. Sure, I was used to talking to a roomful of third graders, but that was no big deal. If you mess up, what are they going to say? Besides, third graders don't judge — grown people do. I must have stood at that podium for a solid minute without saying a word.

Finally I started telling my story. I began with the dying part, because I figured telling my heaven story first would buy God another ten minutes or so to spare me. When I got to the part about the little girl, I started crying, because I knew I was only seconds away from having to explain why God showed me my younger self. I was about to share my most shameful secrets with thirty total strangers. I was crying so hard I had to put my hands over my face. *This is it, God. Now or never. Please don't make me do this.*

Nothing but silence.

I took my hands from my face and caught a glimpse of Virgil standing in the back of the church. He'd left JP in charge of the kids so he could hear my speech. It was at that moment when I saw Virgil that I knew God wasn't going to intervene. So I closed my eyes and put my hands back over my face, and through my sobs I began to talk. And that is how I testified — a blubbery, blotchy mess with shaky hands covering my face.

For the next fifteen minutes, it all came out. The sexual abuse, the feelings of worthlessness, the abortion. Things I'd kept hidden for so long, this enormous chain of secrets and shame that had enslaved me most of my life — all of it came tumbling out. And as I spoke, a thought formed in my head.

They think you're horrible.

Still, I kept going. What else could I do? I kept my eyes closed and my hands on my face the whole time, and it's amazing anyone could even hear a word I said. When

I finished, I heard some polite applause, but I didn't care what anyone thought. All I wanted to do was grab my family and get out of there.

I made a beeline for the exit, and I was only steps away from a clean getaway when a woman blocked my path. She looked at me with a big smile on her face, and she thanked me for coming. Then she took a step toward me. Then another. Before I knew it she had her arms wrapped around me.

She was hugging me.

I looked over her shoulder as she kept holding me, and I couldn't believe what I saw: a long line of women, waiting for their hugs.

One by one they came up and thanked me and embraced me. They told me how much they appreciated my honesty and how much they loved hearing about heaven. All kinds of women. Young and old. A woman with cerebral palsy. A grandmother in her eighties with crazy frizzy hair. Businesswomen in sharp suits. I could hardly believe what was happening. All the judgment and indifference I'd been expecting was just absent from this tiny little church. Instead, there was joy and thanks and a kind of electricity.

Pauline later told me she'd never felt so much energy in one of her church groups.

And then the lady with the frizzy hair said, "That light that was next to you was *so* beautiful." My first thought was, *Huh?* Yes, I'd asked God to stand beside me, but had He actually done it? I wasn't skeptical — after all, God brought me to heaven, so standing next to me in a tiny church couldn't be all that hard. But I did feel overwhelmed by it all, so I let her comment sort of drop and moved on.

Before I knew it, two more women came up to me. They were in their thirties and attractive and smartly dressed in business skirts and jackets. The first one thanked me and gave me a quick hug, but when the second one hugged me, she just wouldn't let go. She held on and pulled me tighter, and I could hear her start to cry. I didn't know what was going on.

The woman finally broke our embrace and looked at me with red eyes.

"I have never told anyone this," she said in a soft voice, "but when I was younger I had an abortion. And I knew God could never forgive me for it. But then I heard you talk today. And now I know if He could forgive you, then He can forgive me, too."

Now it was me who was crying. A sudden

303

wave of love and insight washed over me, as if something magnificent had just been revealed. I looked at this beautiful woman. I saw how she was broken, and I saw how God's love had begun to heal her — right there, right in front of my eyes!

"It's you!" I blurted out. "You are the whole reason He made me do this! God loves you so, so much!"

I finally realized what was happening. God hadn't done this to punish me or embarrass me or make me look like an idiot. He did it because He knew my story would help others who'd been through the same thing — help them break their own chains of shame and secrets. "For it is by grace you have been saved, through faith," it says in Ephesians 2:8–9, "and this is not of yourselves, it is the gift of God." All the torment I'd been feeling inside, all the misgivings and apprehension, all of it just washed clean away. *This* was why He sent me back. *This* was why He had me tell my whole story. If a sinner like me could be forgiven, then *anyone* could be forgiven. God loves all His children, each and every one. This was the message my story was meant to convey.

I finally understood.

It was only later that I realized what song had been playing right after I finished my talk. It was an artist named Chris Tomlin, singing a beautiful song called "Amazing Grace (My Chains Are Gone)."

Just as I was getting ready to sort of float out the front door, I noticed a group of people down by the altar. They were gathered around an older woman in her seventies who was leaning against a walker and crying. They all had their hands on her, and they were praying.

One of the women in the group came up to me and said, "You need to see this."

I walked up behind the woman with the walker. She was crying so hard, she was almost slumped on her walker. When she became aware I was there, she turned as much as she could and looked over her shoulder at me.

"I am seventy-five years old," she said. "And when I was five years old my grandfather started molesting me."

My heart skipped a beat. The woman braced herself against her walker and went on.

"I tried to tell my mother what happened, and she told me to be quiet. I tried to tell other people, and they all told me to be quiet. And I was so mad at God, because I couldn't understand why He didn't help me. And the only answer I could come up with was that He didn't love me. I lived my whole life thinking God didn't love me."

Tears were running down her face. Tears were running down mine.

"And now I know!" she said, her voice breaking. "Now I know God *does* love me! God has loved me all along!"

The woman gave her life to Jesus Christ that day, and she was changed.

I walked out of the church and stood in the bright sunlight. The only words I could think to say were, "Oh, God."

CHAPTER SEVENTEEN

What happened in that church changed everything.

But, like I said, just because you've been to heaven doesn't mean you stop being human. Even after seeing how my talk affected those women, I was *still* leery about telling my story to too many people. Maybe that was just me being selfish, but I still worried about how people would react.

So, for a few weeks after my talk, I was pretty selective about who I opened up to. I didn't just grab people off the street and say, "Hey, guess what? I died!" I was afraid people we were friendly with would stop hanging out with us, so I was careful not to open the floodgates too early in any friendship.

During this time, Virgil and I invited a couple we'd grown to really like to our home for dinner. Amber was a schoolteacher, like me, and her husband, Brandon, was a talented woodworker and all-around great guy. They were deeply passionate about the love and mercy of God and were completely down to earth. We felt like we'd known them forever.

Amber and Brandon had already heard a condensed version of my story in church, and when they came over, Brandon asked to hear more about it. I hesitated, petrified that telling them my whole story — especially the demonic stuff — would just scare them away. But I also knew it would be hard not to share such an important part of myself with people I considered good friends.

So I took a deep breath and told my whole story. Okay, so I stopped every few minutes to say, "Well, that's it. I'm sure you think we're weird, and we'll never hear from you again." I also said, "I know this is going to sound crazy . . ." probably twenty times. But Amber and Brandon just told me to keep going. So I did.

And when I was done, I asked, "You're not going to stop hanging out with us, are you?"

Amber said, "Oh, gaw, gimme a break. None of this surprises me. Now, you got any ice cream?"

They weren't the least bit put off by my

story or the least bit skeptical. They just accepted it as true, because they already knew that with God anything is possible. From that night forward our friendship only grew stronger.

I couldn't count on everyone being as receptive as Amber and Brandon, though, so I still tried to keep a low profile. A couple of months after my talk, Virgil and I changed churches, because we needed a place that had a youth program. We picked a local non-denominational church housed in an old movie theater. The lobby still had a glass counter and a popcorn machine, which made it pretty popular with the younger worshippers. What Virgil and I loved most was that the church was so full of life. We'd both grown up in denominational churches, which gave us a great foundation. But I'd never been to a church where people worshipped God so openly during a service. It was *how* they worshipped that really moved me — their excitement reminded me of how I felt when I was in the presence of God. They were not embarrassed to raise their hands and praise God and even cry. I remember thinking, *Gee, these people didn't even die and see God, and they still love Him this much.* Virgil and I knew we'd found our new home.

The church had a weekly Life Group, which is pretty much what its name says it is — a group of people sitting around sharing their lives, their joys and prayers, their struggles, and funny jokes. I loved the idea, and Virgil and I signed up for Wednesday nights. On our way to our first one, I told Virgil, "Don't tell anyone about what happened to me." He understood I didn't want to draw attention to myself in that first meeting, and he promised he wouldn't mention it.

About a half hour into the meeting, the topic turned to what it would be like to be in the presence of God. One of the members, a lovely woman named Diane, got teary eyed and said, "I can only imagine what it must be like to stand with God." I bit my lip and looked over at Virgil, as if to say, "Remember, mum's the word." But Diane kept talking and wondering what God was like, and her passion and yearning to know was just amazing. It was all I could do not to jump to my feet and launch into my story. Just then, I heard a man's voice.

"You know, my wife died and went to heaven," Virgil said sheepishly.

Way to keep that poker face, hubby.

It turned out my fears were unfounded. Diane and her husband, Rudy, immediately leaned forward, and Diane rubbed her hands together and said, "Ooh, tell us about it." Everyone in the group was excited to hear me talk. I gave a shortened version of my story, but that wasn't enough for Diane. She made me hand over my phone number, and the next day we got together and I gave her the full account. I was sure if I told her the whole story, her excitement would die down. But it didn't. She began reading me scriptures about spiritual warfare, and she became one of my great friends and a spiritual mentor.

Diane also brought me over to meet our pastor's wife, Opal, in her home. Opal has fiery red hair and a smile that melts your heart. She's colorful and outspoken, and, honestly, I was a little intimidated by her. I'd grown to love our new church, and as usual I worried that my story would make her think I was strange and maybe even ask us to leave. I was so nervous, I started to shake and cry.

Opal gave me one of her no-nonsense looks.

"Why are you so afraid?"

I didn't know how to answer her, which was fine because she didn't wait for an answer.

"Fear is not of God," she told me. "The

authority rests with God."

Opal was very matter-of-fact. She listened to my story, and we talked about it for a bit. She gave me wonderful advice, and then, just like that, she got up and said, "Ladies, I gotta go. I have a hair appointment."

I remember thinking, *Wow, whatever it is she has, I want it.* I was mesmerized by her spiritual strength. Opal was just so confident about God, so sure of His power and His grace. Nothing could faze her, not even the demonic stuff that always seemed to rattle me. The best way I can describe it is to say that Opal *poured* the truth right into me. She helped me to see that it didn't matter what anyone on Earth thought about my story. I knew every word of what I was saying was true, and I had to stop worrying about people's reactions — plain and simple! Opal's faith and conviction were so reassuring, and I think I took a step closer to my own authority in Christ that night.

It was great when people reacted positively to my story, but there were times when that didn't happen. There were times when I believed people were put in my path to hear my story, only to have them tell me it had no relevance for them.

312

"Thank you so much for sharing. I definitely believe you, but I don't know why you were supposed to share this with me," one woman told me before getting up and walking away.

Another time, I noticed someone standing near me, and I felt one of those powerful nudges — *this woman needs your testimony.* I still wasn't all that comfortable in my role as the "heaven lady," but there was no denying this nudge. So I approached her and told her my story.

"Crystal, wow, I love that story, but I'm not sure why you think you were supposed to tell it to me," she said when I finished.

I couldn't believe it happened again. Wasn't my purpose to share my story with people who needed to hear it? I apologized to the woman and said good-bye. *God,* I thought, *You're making me look like a real idiot.*

A few months later, out of the blue, I got a phone call from the first woman, who told me she needed to talk. "You were right," she said when we got together. "There *was* a reason I needed to hear your story." While we talked I could see how broken she was — the same way I'd been broken. And I could also see how God's message had helped her rip away her own awful curtain

313

of shame. It had taken her a while to work it all out, but she was in the process of being spiritually healed.

So God knew what He was doing after all, I thought. *How about that?*

Not much later, I got a call from the second woman. She told me pretty much the same thing: that when she heard my story, she panicked and denied it had any relevance for her. But actually it did, and hearing it made her realize that God had never stopped loving her, no matter what had happened in her past.

After years and years of secrecy and shame, she too was free.

After that, I never questioned one of God's nudges again.

The nudges happen at totally random times, usually when it's not especially convenient. I'll be out shopping with my kids, and suddenly I'll feel the nudge: *Tell this person; they need to hear it.* It doesn't happen every day, but a few times a week is not uncommon. I've done it so often that Virgil and the children are no longer surprised to see me stop in my tracks and start yammering away about heaven — though sometimes the kids get a little weirded out by it. One time, Sabyre and I were in the checkout line at a supermarket when I got a nudge to tell the woman standing behind us. Mind you, there were a whole bunch of people in line, and this woman was just minding her own business, sifting through coupons. Hardly an ideal time for a heart-to-heart about how I died. But I'd learned not to ignore the nudges. So I turned around and started a conversation.

Sabyre saw right away what was happening and said, "Mom, I'm just gonna wait over there." She knew from experience this was going to take a while, and she figured she'd better find a comfy place to sit.

Another time we were in one of our favorite hamburger joints, a place called Meers in Comanche County. Awesome longhorn burgers and frickles (that's fried pickles, in case you've never tried them). Our food had just arrived when I noticed three elderly women sitting at the table behind us. I got a nudge about one of them, and I thought, *Really? Now? My burger just got here!* But, again, I knew better than to argue with God. I waited for an opening and swooped in.

"Hey there," I said. "Where y'all from?"

It turned out we knew the woman's husband. That was all I needed to hear.

"I know this is gonna sound crazy," I said,

"but in 2009 I died and went to heaven."

The woman looked at me with a totally blank expression. I knew this was the moment when it could go either way. After a few seconds, she said, "Would you mind coming over and telling us about it?" I joined them at their table and told them my story, and halfway through I could see the woman's eyes start to well up. That was my validation. God was right again.

"You know," the woman said when I was done, "I was abused as a child."

"Me, too," I heard, and I looked at her friend. She was crying, too.

Wow, two for one. Nice work, God.

There was only one downside. When I got back to our table, I saw that Virgil had eaten my hamburger.

That's happened to me a lot in the past few months. I like to think of it as the God diet.

Some of the nudges have led to truly amazing encounters. In 2011, I attended a Christian women's conference not far from my hometown, and on my first day I found myself wandering around the cafeteria carrying my tray and looking for a place to sit. I knew a few women at the conference, but their tables were full. The only open seat I could see was at a table with several young women I'd never met. So I took that seat, kept my head down, and quietly picked up my fork.

I was just about to take my first bite when I got the nudge: *Tell her.*

I looked up and saw a pretty young woman across the table. She was in her early twenties, with lovely brown hair down to her shoulders. I thought, *Oh, God, no, please. I'm at a table of strangers. How am I supposed to do this? How do I bring it up?* I felt my face turning red.

Even so, I put down my fork, took a breath, and looked straight at the woman.

"So," I said to her, "in 2009 I died and went to heaven, and God wants me to tell you about it."

The woman looked a little startled and said, "Uh . . . okay."

So I told her my story. She wasn't directly across from me, so there were other women at the table overhearing us, which made me feel more embarrassed. But I just kept saying how much God loved her — how very, very much He loved her — and no matter what she had done or what was done to her, His love would not fail her. That's when she began to cry.

God was right again. Well, He always is.

Later, when we were alone, the young woman came clean.

"I've only told this to one other person in my life and not even my mother," she said, "but when I was young my stepfather sexually abused me." She had never talked openly about what happened; instead, she hid it deep inside, probably believing she'd keep it a secret until she died. But then on this day the love of God shattered the secret, and the chains were loosened. Her healing had begun. I don't know if she would have eventually told her story to someone, but I do know that God put me in a room with her so He could convey to her how very much He loved her.

There is also the story of Patricia, a special ed teacher I worked with. She is vibrant, funny, and incredibly kind, and I love having her as a friend. A few years before I met her, her teenage daughter Heather was killed in a car accident. I knew about it, but it wasn't anything we ever really talked about.

I hadn't seen Patricia in a while when I brought Willow, who was around one, to see her at her school. Patricia was standing in the hallway by the cafeteria while her students were up onstage practicing for a Mother's Day pageant. They were singing

318

Josh Groban's "You Raise Me Up," a beautiful song about how God lifts us when we're down. When Patricia looked over and saw us, I could tell she was crying. It seemed like the lyrics of the song were really getting to her.

Then something strange and remarkable happened. Willow is a sweet little girl who likes to stick her nose in everything and approaches life with a natural curiosity, but even so, she isn't that comfortable meeting new people. When it comes to strangers, she's a little guarded, which is why I was so surprised when, the moment Willow noticed Patricia was crying, she suddenly lunged and threw her skinny little arms around her.

Patricia was stunned. She closed her eyes and hugged Willow back, and they held on to each other like that for the longest time. While they hugged I could hear the little children singing their beautiful song — a song about how, when hard times come: "I am still and wait here in the silence / Until you come and sit awhile with me."

Only when the song was finished did Willow let go and reach back for me, like nothing extraordinary had happened. I went over and hugged Patricia myself.

"That was the song we played at Heather's funeral," she told me.

Now I knew why she was crying, but I still couldn't understand the connection to Willow. Then Patricia continued.

"After the funeral, we planted a tree in Heather's memory," she said. "And it was a willow tree."

God's hand at work or coincidence? You'd think by then I wouldn't ever have to ask myself that question, but occasionally I still do. I saw with my own eyes how Willow had given my friend such great comfort just when she needed it most by doing something I'd never seen Willow do before. And the song? And the tree? If that was a coincidence, it was one heck of a coincidence.

After that happened, I got a strong nudge to tell Patricia my story. I messaged her online and told her I needed to talk, and we agreed to meet at a little coffee shop in town. On my way over, I started worrying. I'd almost gotten to the point where I didn't care if people thought I was a wackadoodle — almost. I prayed and asked God if He was sure I needed to tell her my story. And then, for some reason, I asked God if there was anything I could tell her to let her know I was telling the truth. Because if she knew I was telling the truth, she'd know her daughter was okay.

Just then, the words "blue rabbit" formed in my head.

I thought, *Okay, tell her "blue rabbit,"* but then I thought, *No, don't tell her that. That's crazy. For one thing, there's no such thing as a blue rabbit. It's just a silly, nonsensical thing that popped in my brain. Forget it, don't mention it to her. Just tell her your story and go.*

But then, in the coffee shop, I felt the urge to tell Patricia about the blue rabbit. I decided to lie and say it was something that came to me in a dream. Just before I launched into my heaven story, I said, "You know, I had this crazy dream last night where Heather told me to tell you 'blue rabbit,' as a way to let you know she's okay. Isn't that weird?" I said it kind of offhandedly, so it wouldn't seem like a big deal.

Patricia sat there stone-faced, saying nothing, showing nothing. I immediately felt stupid.

"Dreams are so dumb," I said. "I'm sorry I brought it up."

And then I told her my story. When I was done, Patricia was silent and stone-faced again. Finally, she looked at me, and she spoke.

"Heather's favorite color was blue," she said. "And her favorite animals were rabbits. And on her grandfather's farm we have these floppy-eared rabbits we're raising in Heather's memory. She loved rabbits so much we called her Honey Bunny."

Patricia was crying now, and so was I.

"Heather also had this old stuffed rabbit she loved and slept with every night," she said. "Crystal, that old stuffed rabbit was blue."

Our God is a God of love and mercy and forgiveness and great power, and in His mercy He can do truly astonishing things. So I don't know why I'd be the least bit surprised that God could send me the words "blue rabbit." And yet, whenever something like that happens, I'm always blown away. I guess I'll never get used to how great God is.

I was in the flower aisle at Walmart when another amazing encounter happened. I was holding Micah, and Virgil was over by the azaleas with Willow. Just then I saw an acquaintance, Shearl, pushing her son Mickey in his wheelchair. Mickey, who was in his twenties, had been severely injured in a car accident. Shearl and I made some small talk before she said, "You know, sometime I'd really like to hear your story."

Usually I would have said, "sure, anytime," but for some reason I blurted out, "How about now?"

There are times when, if the situation calls for it, I'll abridge my story a bit. I might just say that when I was younger, I felt really worthless, instead of going into all the details of my abortion. But in this case, I had the urge to tell them everything. And so I did, right there in the flower aisle. I handed Micah over to Virgil, and I gave Shearl and her son the unabridged version.

Toward the end of it, when I was talking about how great God is, Mickey started to cry. Then he was crying uncontrollably. Something I said must have really affected him.

"You gonna be okay, Mickey?" Shearl asked him. "Do you want Crystal to stop?"

I heard Mickey push out the words, "No. Keep talking."

So I did. And when I was done, Shearl hugged me and thanked me and said, "We are believers. We believe in a God of healing and miracles." Shearl explained that when Mickey was taken to the hospital after his accident, she came very close to losing him. His heart stopped twice, and he was revived both times.

Then Mickey looked up at me with tears running down his face and struggled to speak again.

"But I didn't see God," he said in his broken voice. "I didn't see God."

My heart swelled with love for him. It swelled with God's love for him. I knelt down and got eye level with him and put my hands on his.

"Mickey, I don't have all the answers," I said. "I don't know why you had to go through what you did. I don't know why your accident happened or why you have to struggle, but I do know one thing. God's plan is perfect. It was through the trash in my life that God glorified Himself the most."

And then I added, "God is real. He is real."

I said that again. And again. Over and over.

Mickey never took his eyes off me. Then I asked if I could pray over him. There in the flower aisle I laid my hands on Mickey, and Shearl put her hands on him, too. And as shoppers passed and gave us funny looks, we glorified God's presence in our lives, praying for healing for Mickey and thanking God for meeting us in the aisles of our local Walmart.

Shearl would later tell me my talk meant a great deal to Mickey. He is a remarkable young man who believes with all his heart that God is going to let him walk again, and no one who knows him doubts that he will. But in his darker moments his faith is tested, as it is with all of us.

"Sometimes," Shearl said, "people need to be reminded that God is real."

I've thought about Mickey a lot since our talk in the flower aisle, and I think he made me realize a very profound truth about my experience. In fact, that truth is at the very heart of God's message to us. Yes, God gave me the miraculous gift of His presence and His wisdom, and because of my time in heaven I now overflow with excitement and passion for Him. The love I felt pass between us changed me forever. I am beyond lucky to have had this experience, and I can't even imagine what my life would be like if I hadn't.

But here's the thing — *you don't have to die and go to heaven to experience God.*

Look at Mickey. He was in the same spot I was in — in a hospital, teetering between life and death — and yet he didn't get to see God. But still, he loves God with every fiber of his being, and he believes God will help him walk again. His passion is every bit as great as mine, and maybe even greater, and he didn't even get to stand in God's presence! Mickey's incredible faith touches my heart and stirs my soul, and he is not the only one. I have seen that burning passion in other Christians who didn't need to go to heaven to know that God is real — to love Him mightily and be His warrior on Earth.

Which brings me to my great friend Amber.

Amber's passion for God blows me away. She's young and beautiful and full of life, and all the kids in her fourth-grade class just love her to death. She also mentors a bunch of teenage girls, and people call her the Teen Whisperer. When you're around her you see what a living, breathing thing her faith is. What Amber understands, and what she has helped me understand, is that *everyone* has a story — *everyone* has a testimony. Every one of us is born in sin and endures pain and suffering, and every one of us can be freed from that burden when we realize we are more — *so much more* — than just that pain and suffering. When we see the greatness of God in even our very darkest moments, then we can be free. "Even the crappiest crap we go through glorifies God," Amber likes to say, in her Amber way. "God makes beauty from ashes, and the devil hates when He does that."

God has made beauty from the ashes of Amber's life. She has seen His greatness in her darkest moments. Amber proves every day you don't have to die and go to heaven to believe in God and be His warrior, and for that reason I asked Amber if she would share her testimony — her amazingly personal and powerful testimony — with you. She agreed.

Amber is a Texas girl, and from a very early age she knew she was filled with the Holy Spirit. But, like me, she had a rough childhood. She grew up in an atmosphere of chaos and dysfunction. Through it all, she had a desire to live her life for God, because deep down she knew she was created for more than what she was growing up with. And so she fought off all the hardships that were testing her faith. While all the other high school freshman girls were smoking and drinking and having sex and even trying drugs, Amber stayed away from all that. She went to a party here and there, but she was always the designated driver.

Then, toward the end of her freshman year, she gave in to the pressures of life. She allowed the bitterness and resentment she felt about her situation to turn into blatant rebellion. She quit cheerleading and missed so much school that she had to go to court twice. She smoked pot and became promiscuous. She popped pills and went on drinking binges. She got into physical fights with her mother and moved out when she was seventeen. She let the anger inside her — and the lies of the enemy — drag her down.

In her senior year, she got pregnant.

Amber didn't believe in abortion. In the fourth grade, when all the students wrote letters to President Clinton, hers got published in a newspaper. Most kids told the president how much they liked him or how much they wanted to visit the White House; Amber wrote about her belief that life begins at conception. Even so, when she got pregnant, she feared that having a child that young would doom her to the kind of life her parents had — to poverty and fighting and unhappiness. She believed the lie that she could have an abortion and never look back. Against all of her instincts, she rounded up $450 in cash and went to an abortion clinic in a town three hours away, crying in the backseat the whole way up. She didn't tell anyone about it except her mom and her boyfriend, but when her eleven-year-old sister, Lacey, overheard her talking about it, she prayed and prayed that the abortion wouldn't work.

Amber sat in the clinic waiting room with

its circular couches and magazine racks. She sat near the front door, away from everyone else. She felt the same instinct I felt: *Get up and go home now.* But her body seemed like it weighed a million pounds. She went through with the abortion and walked out into the harsh sunlight afterward feeling deeply ashamed. She didn't go to school for a week. She lay in bed and cried and slept and cried.

But one month later, Amber noticed she wasn't getting her period. She'd broken up with her boyfriend and stopped having sex, so she was pretty confused. She took a pregnancy test just to make sure she wasn't still pregnant. The test result was positive.

She *was* pregnant.

I'll let Amber take the story from here.

I knew this had to be some kind of mistake. It wasn't like I was the Virgin Mary or anything. I really didn't understand what was happening. After I took the test I lay in my bed all night and cried in fear and confusion. As I lay there, I noticed a little lump in my belly. I touched it a couple of times, and I felt several small, quick flutters. Looking back now, I realize God allowed me to feel those flutters, because He knew I hadn't convinced myself that

329

what was growing inside me was a child. In that moment, in my bed, it was like God was telling me, "You cannot deny that I am the giver of life."

But I was still really scared and confused, and I got my mom to take me to the ER in Amarillo. I got a sonogram, which showed I was fourteen weeks pregnant — and that the baby seemed fine.

I called the abortion clinic to find out what happened, and they said they'd never seen anything like this before. They said maybe it was twins, and we only got one. But I didn't really need any answers from them. I knew what was happening. This was God giving me a second chance.

But then, at twenty weeks, I woke up in a pool of blood. My mom rushed me back to the ER. At twenty-one weeks, I went into labor. The doctors told me my early labor was the result of a bicornuate uterus I was born with and didn't have anything to do with the abortion. They also told me my baby wasn't viable, that it had zero chances to survive. I didn't want to hear it. Right in the middle of labor I got out of bed and on my knees and prayed to God to let me keep this child.

After ten hours of labor, I gave birth to a daughter. The child was alive but struggling to breathe. She was less than a foot long, and she weighed fifteen ounces.

The nurses took my baby to the nursery, cut and pieced a tiny triangular piece of cloth on her as a diaper, and wrapped her in a pink-and-blue-striped blanket. Then they put her in an incubator. All the nurses were surprised my baby was even alive. One of the nurses asked me if I wanted to hold her. In my emotional agony, I pushed out a "no." It wasn't that I didn't want to hold her; it's just that in those moments I thought, This is it, God, this is what's going to break me. This I can't handle. There is no way I can hold her and love her and then let her be taken away. I'd had to deal with so much garbage in my life, and now this? I was filled with anger and resentment toward God. What kind of God would toy with me like this? Wasn't this supposed to be my second chance?

In a blur, my family and friends came and went, giving me their love and support. My best friend Lauren, who knew me so well, didn't say a word. She just curled up on the end of my bed and lay there with me. And all that time, my younger sister, Lacey, was nearby in the nursery, holding my tiny daughter. Lacey, who had prayed for weeks for my baby to live, was experiencing the joy and the gift of an answered prayer.

A nurse asked again if I wanted to hold my baby, and again I said no. No one thought she could survive much longer, and I didn't want to look at her and then never see her again. My friends and family filed into the nursery, saying their good-byes to the child. I just lay in my room in total silence. I was done, finished, at my breaking point.

I didn't even realize it, but thirty minutes had now passed since my baby was born. Somehow she was still hanging on. That's when a grief counselor came over to talk to me.

"Amber, I want you to think really hard about this," she said. "Years from now, are you going to regret not holding your daughter?"

In a flash, I realized she was right.

"Oh, my God, yes, I'll hold her!" I yelled out. A nurse brought my baby to me bundled in her pink-and-blue blanket.

I couldn't believe how tiny and fragile she was. She wasn't much bigger than the palm of my hand, and her body and limbs were so skinny. But I was surprised she looked like a baby — a perfect baby that happened to be too little. I could hear her taking these tiny, gasping breaths for air. A nurse told me this was because her lungs weren't developed. I just held her and stared at her and loved her. And as I lifted up parts of the blanket to gaze over this perfect little creation, one thought flooded my mind: This is the life I tried to end.

In the pain and grief of that moment I didn't understand that God was showing me His redemptive love.

And then I heard my daughter take one last tiny gasp for air.

I handed her back to the nurse, who carried her out of the room. Just a bit later the nurse came back to my room and held my hand.

"Amber," she said, "she is gone to be with Jesus."

My baby hung on for forty-two minutes — just long enough for me to hold her.

I don't have all the answers, but I do know that God gave me a second chance to see His mighty hand create beauty from ashes. I know that those few minutes with my daughter changed my life. They added another beautiful part to my purpose and destiny. My daughter showed me a real love — the true love of my Father. And now I would never give back any of the pain and suffering and grief I felt, because it all led to that blessed miracle — when I got to hold my daughter for those few minutes.

Through it all, God showed me He holds the key to life and death. He took away my crippling shame and sorrow and replaced it with the powerful truth of His redemption. There is so much I still don't understand about God. There are times when I still wrestle with Him, but in the end I always come back to the truth of knowing that He is good. He showed me I am more than the pain and suffering in my life. I am His perfect creation, and He is always there. He is my redemptive love.

And now my baby is part of my testimony.

Her name is Kylie Ryan.

CHAPTER EIGHTEEN

Just a couple of months before I started writing this book, I attended a Christian conference in Oklahoma City. I really enjoyed getting together with other Christians and talking about our lives. Not surprisingly, I shared my story a handful of times over three days. On the last night of the conference, a woman who'd heard my testimony asked if I wouldn't mind dropping by her hotel room and telling my story to a few friends. I said, sure, I'd be happy to stop by. Three or four people I could handle.

When I walked into her room, I could barely squeeze through the door. Every inch of the place was packed. It was a pretty small area, with two twin beds, a bunk bed in the corner, and a chair or two — and people were sitting on every available surface, including the carpeted floor. There were women of all ages, some in their sixties, some in their teens, all of them looking at me with expectant faces. There were five teenagers hanging off the top bunk bed. I didn't count, but there had to be at least twenty-five women crammed in that little space.

I remember thinking, *Oh, dear.*

True to form, my heart started racing and my face got blotchy. But I took a deep breath and made it through my story. I cried a lot, especially during the abortion part. "I'm not crying out of regret," I told everyone. "I'm crying out of sadness for the lost girl I was."

Right in the middle of it, my friend Amber walked in eating a bowl of ice cream. "Wow, it stinks in here," she said. "What are y'all talking about?" When she saw me, she figured it out and smiled.

"Oh, gaw, I already heard that a bunch of times," Amber said, winking at me. "See ya."

I think she wanted to get me used to telling my story without her around.

When I finally finished, it was nearly 1:00 a.m. I headed for the door, and a woman jumped in my path. I was getting used to women jumping in my path.

"Excuse me, Crystal, do you have a second to talk?" she asked. Her lips were quivering and her eyes were filling with tears. I knew what was coming.

"I've never talked about this with anyone," she said. "*Anyone.* So it's really hard for me to even say this out loud."

Lay it on me, sister, I thought. *Let it out.*

"When I was younger," she finally said, "I was sexually abused."

We spoke for several minutes, and then we prayed together. "The enemy wants you to keep it a secret," I told her. "The enemy loves secrets and shame." I've since found out she now gives talks about her experience to other women who have been abused. The circle of salvation is widening. Chains are being broken everywhere.

I was already on way to my own room when another young woman, Kelli, stopped me. "I know this sounds crazy," she said, "but when you were talking, I couldn't see your face anymore."

"What do you mean?"

"All I could see was this bright light around your face. It was like this golden glow."

I'd heard this before — from the frizzy-haired woman in Thomas who said she'd seen a beautiful light by my side — but I hadn't given it much thought. And now I looked for an explanation, like the glare of a lamp bouncing off a mirror or something. I prayed with Kelli for a few minutes and finally made it to bed.

But the next day, another young woman approached me and said, "Crystal, I couldn't see your face when you were talking. There was just this light all over it."

In all, three women who were in the room that night told me they couldn't see my face. All they could see was a bright golden light.

I knew what they'd seen was a glimpse of God's presence, and that made me cry. To be honest, I cried because I was jealous. I was jealous because they got to see God. I know, I know, I got to be in His presence, so what right did I have to be jealous? But the fact is, once I met God, I knew I'd be chasing Him for the rest of my life.

Many people who hear my story ask me the same question: "Why did God choose you?"

I've given that plenty of thought since 2009, and the best answer I've come up with is, why not me?

What I mean by that is, there's nothing special about me at all. God didn't say, "Oh, there goes Crystal. Isn't she something?" I'm certainly not better than anyone else, and I'm also not worse. I'm a mom and a wife and a schoolteacher in a small Oklahoma town. I am ordinary in every way. Who knows? Maybe God thought, *Boy, she sure does like to talk, so if I can get her to talk about Me, she'll never shut up.* And if He thought that, well, He was right.

But the truth is, I really don't know why God gave me this gift. I don't know why I saw what I saw while others who have died and come back saw nothing. And honestly, I don't need to know. I may not always understand God's plan, but I do know that it's perfect.

And anyway, it's not important why God chose me, because what happened isn't really *about* me. And the lights all those women saw around me? Those aren't about me, either. Those lights are about God. My story, and my testimony, is all about God. Everything I've gone through in my life is all about God. This book is a book about *God and His presence in our lives.*

So when I say, "Why not me?" I mean that I'm just like anyone else who has ever searched for God. I'm like anyone who has ever longed to feel God's presence. For all the doubt and skepticism that kept me tied up in knots for years, I can honestly say I never stopped looking for God. I never stopped yearning for a relationship with Him. Even in my darkest moments, when I vowed to cut God out of my life, I never really did. I just kept talking to Him, and He kept pursuing me.

I was talking, and He heard every word. And He was talking, but I couldn't hear a thing.

Maybe He picked me, because He got tired of me not listening.

But here's the thing — *God talks to all of us.*

Yes, God was there with me at my speeches. But God is there with all of us, always, no matter what we're doing. You don't have to see a glowing light to know that God is with you. You don't have to die and go to heaven to know you are in His presence. All you have to do is want to have a relationship with Him. All you have to do is *look* for Him. "Seek and you will find," it says in Matthew 7:7. "Knock and the door will be opened to you."

I did a lot of seeking and knocking. And finally I found Him. Or maybe more accurately, He found me.

I can't wait to tell everyone that God is real. But what I've found as I've gone out and told my story is that, more often the not, the people I think I'm ministering to are actually ministering to me. I think I'm teaching them about God. Instead, they're teaching me about faith.

I'll give you an example. When the twins were in the NICU, we had a lot people praying for them every day. A woman who worked with my mom, Danica, and her husband, Danny, who was a pastor in another small town, came by the hospital one day to pray over the twins. A nurse told them they weren't allowed to enter the NICU. They could have just left, but they didn't.

Instead, they laid their hands on the metal door that led into the NICU, and they prayed for the twins right there.

Not much later, we learned Danny was gravely ill. Virgil and I prayed hard for him, just as he'd prayed for our twins. But then, one day when I was sitting in a doctor's office, I felt another nudge from God. He wanted me to do more than just pray for Danny — He wanted me to give him $600. Now, the school year was just about to start for my two older kids, so we needed to buy new shoes and supplies. And our mortgage was due, and we had other bills, and we just didn't have a dollar to spare. But here was God anyway, telling me to send Danny money. I called Virgil and told him about the nudge, and, as always, he didn't hesitate.

"Just write the check," he said. I couldn't understand where the money was going to come from, and I sat there in the doctor's office and prayed to God to help me understand.

Just then — *just then* — I got a text message from a woman from my church. She'd never sent me a text before, and the text simply read, "Hebrews 11:1." That was it, nothing else — just the scripture. I found a Bible in the doctor's waiting room and quickly opened it to the passage. What I read astonished me.

"Now faith is the substance of things hoped for and the evidence of things unseen" (KJV).

Out of the blue, my friend had sent me a message about faith. I immediately knew this was God talking to me again. While I was sitting there grappling with His instructions, He sent me a simple message — *have faith in Me.* That night, we sent Danny the money.

Only a few months later, Danny took a turn for the worse. He was losing weight fast, and he didn't have long to live. Virgil and I went to see him, and I held Danny's hand as we sat with him and his wife and prayed. I told him how much it meant to us that he and his wife had prayed over our twins in the hospital. And Danny, in his weakened voice, told me what it had meant to him when he received the money from us.

"We were in need, and I was praying and praying," he said. "And then you sent us exactly what we needed. God answered our prayers."

I sat there and thought, *God used me to help Danny.* But, like I said, whenever I think I am ministering to someone, they are actually ministering to me.

At one point during our visit with Danny, he looked at me and asked, "What is heaven like?"

I told him what it felt like to be with God. I described the almost unbearable joy I felt at seeing my younger self. Then I said, "You know, Danny, God took me before I felt an ounce of pain. There was no suffering. There was only joy."

When I told him this, Danny smiled and turned to his wife. He didn't say anything to her, and he didn't have to. Danica was crying, not out of sadness but out of relief. "That's what I've been worried about the most," she said through her tears. "I can't bear the thought of Danny suffering."

Danny drew comfort from what I told him, but not for himself — he drew it for his wife. He didn't even ask me about heaven for himself; he did that for Danica, too. He wanted her to know that, at the very end when his mind and body failed and he was at his most vulnerable, she didn't have to suffer for him because he'd already be gone. He'd already be on his way to heaven.

What a great lesson in faith and love! How remarkable that God never stops ministering to me. The strength of Danny's belief in God filled me with hope and inspiration. But God wasn't done yet. As Virgil and I were leaving, I noticed a beautiful cross on the wall. I told Danny how much I liked it, and he said, "That's my favorite scripture." I hadn't seen any scripture, just the cross. But then his wife stepped out of the way, and I saw a verse printed just to the side of the cross:

"Now faith is the substance of things hoped for and the evidence of things unseen."

It was Hebrews 11:1 yet again. And today, that verse is stenciled on my wall at home. I put it there to remind me of how Danny ministered to me in his last days of life, and I think of him every time I pass it.

God turns the tables on me all the time. When I think I'm teaching, I'm actually learning. Whenever I talk to my great friend

Amber, I always get back much more than I give. When I spoke with Patricia about her daughter Heather, her faith in the face of such a terrible loss really touched my heart. Then there was Shearl and her brave son Mickey. Shearl would later explain to me that when she saw me in Walmart, she felt a strange urge to go over and talk to me. She shrugged it off and walked past me but then circled back. She passed and circled two more times before finally giving in to the urge.

So while I thought God put me in the flower aisle to talk to them, He actually put them there to talk to me.

Why? Because of Mickey.

Mickey is, in ways I can only admire, God's warrior. He was ejected from a truck and suffered a broken back and severe brain trauma. If the first responder had shown up even a minute later, Mickey would have died on the road. He was in a coma for three weeks, and doctors told Shearl he probably wouldn't make it. But on the day doctors told Mickey's family to gather up and say good-bye to him, they instead gathered up and prayed to God to save Mickey's life. They spoke life over him with scriptures. And within hours, Mickey's condition changed. He pulled through.

Then doctors said he'd probably never talk or laugh — now he does those things, too. And while his life is extremely hard and his battle is sure to be long, Mickey has never once cursed God or doubted God or asked God why this happened to him. All of his pain and suffering has only made him more confident in how much God loves him. Even in the darkest darkness, he feels God's presence.

Beauty from ashes.

Later, when I asked Mickey if it would be okay if I put his story in this book, he didn't hesitate. "Yes," he said. "I want God to use me. I want people to know that the God I worship is a loving God."

There's another question people always ask me: "What does God's voice sound like?"

I don't know if they expect me to say God has a big, booming voice that comes down from the heavens, but it's not like that at all for me. When I hear God's voice — when one of those thoughts pops in my head or I get one of those sudden nudges — what I'm hearing is my own voice. And because it's my own voice, it can get confusing. Early on I used to confuse God's commands with silly, random thoughts, like when I fought so hard not to leave a $100 tip, or when I almost didn't tell Patricia about "blue rabbit." But now I can recognize God's commands, because they're usually something I don't want to do. They're something that will probably embarrass me, and, like I said, I hate to be embarrassed. But that's how I know it's God and not me — He puts me in positions I would never put myself.

That's not to say I don't have internal debates over a thought, because sometimes I still do. And that's because the enemy also uses my voice to talk to me. So I have to stop and ask myself, *If I follow this instinct, is it going to help me or help someone else? Is it of the flesh, or is it of the spirit?* And if you think about it for a while, you can usually figure out that, *No, that is not God. That is of the flesh.* You begin to recognize your own voice, the enemy's voice, and God's voice.

But God doesn't use only words to speak to us. Sometimes it can be a feeling or the sense that you're being drawn to a person or place. And sometimes, God comes to us in our dreams.

Remember I told you about the dream I had where my brother Jayson was singing and worshipping on the stage of a church? When I had the dream, Jayson was in his twenties and struggling mightily. All he felt was a deep resentment for how his childhood had gone and how his life had turned out. He became a hard-core, reckless drinker. He remembers waking up behind the wheel of his truck one night as the truck was barreling 60 miles per hour through a cornfield. Another time, he remembers driving his motorcycle the two hours from Oklahoma City to my hometown in the middle of the night. He was dead drunk, had no helmet on, and drove 130 miles per hour the whole way. He didn't care enough about himself or anyone else to make any changes. He entertained the idea of a lonely, drunken death, and he was okay with it.

Eventually his behavior led to four arrests for driving under the influence. Through it all, Jayson never wavered in his feelings about God. While I was always of two minds — is He real or isn't He? — Jayson would always flat out say, "God doesn't exist." When I'd visit him at his home and try to bring up God, he'd say, "Don't come into my house and talk that hocus-pocus God stuff." And so we never talked about God. But I never forgot my dream, and I clung to the hope that God would find Jayson. Oddly enough, I truly believed He *would* save Jayson, even while I wasn't sure He would ever save me.

Well, today things are different. Today, Jayson stands on the stage of a chapel and sings and worships God — just like in my dream.

How did it happen? Oddly enough, my brother says it happened in a jail cell. He was there after his fourth DUI arrest and was facing ten years in prison. He remembers waking up in the top bunk in the cell. The man in the bottom bunk was a crack addict loudly proclaiming his innocence. The other one, a skinny older man, sat on the floor and quietly read a Bible.

After a while, Jayson got tired of hearing the addict's excuses and explanations for why he failed a drug test. He leaned down from the top bunk and let the guy have it.

"Do you hear yourself, man?" Jayson said. "Listen to yourself! You're here, because you did drugs! You did drugs! It's what you do!"

Just then the old man on the floor spoke for the first time. Jayson remembers he looked like an aging hippie, with smoky glasses and a pirate ship and a compass tattooed on his chest. He reminded Jayson of Jerry Garcia. When Jayson finished haranguing the crack addict, the old man looked at Jayson and said, "Why are *you* here?"

It wasn't a question, and Jayson didn't answer him. He just lay back in his bed and stared at the ceiling. He knew what point the old man was making: who was Jayson to be berating the addict when he was a busted and broken addict himself? Those four words felt like a painful and devastating lesson for Jayson. They left no room for excuses or enabling behavior. They were a call for Jayson to finally take stock of himself and see how utterly wrecked he was.

And right there, in his top bunk, he turned the page on his old life.

The next day guards had the inmates step out of their cells so they could do a head count. When they went back in, Jayson noticed the old man wasn't there. "What happened to the old guy?" he asked the addict. "What old guy?" he said. When Jayson made bond, he asked the guard how many people had been in his cell with him.

"How many bunks do you see, dumbass?" the guard said.

Had the old man been a hallucination? Even during his worst drinking binges Jayson had never hallucinated anything like that. Was it a manifestation of his dire mental state? Or had it been something divine? Jayson didn't know for sure. But what he did know was that he went into prison a broken man, and he came out more whole than he'd ever been in his life. He came out wanting to *change.*

And he did. He went to AA meetings and

stopped drinking. He went to a series of sermons called "Practical Atheists" and realized he wanted a relationship with God. And on November 2, at 12:47 p.m. — he remembers the day and time precisely — Jayson accepted Jesus Christ in his life.

God now comes first in Jayson's life, and he gives God thanks and credit for the woman he calls "my No. 2" — his wife, Melissa. He met her after getting sober and taking a job at the Christian University where she worked. Jayson had no desire to be in a relationship, but God had other plans. Melissa is sweet and tender and strikingly beautiful, and "she has a smile so big it makes other people's cheeks crease," as Jayson likes to say. I've never seen him happier.

Today Jayson leads chapel time at the college where he works, bounding up onstage and leading other worshippers in song — just like in my dream. "Pain and fear can dominate your life for a long time," Jayson says now. "But fear and faith cannot coexist. You have to choose which one you are going to serve, and that's what I did. And now everything I do I try to do for the glory of God."

God saved Jayson from the same darkness He saved me.

The other weird dream I had puzzled me for a long time. It's the one that made me wake up Virgil and tell him I knew God's perfect plan for us, except I could only remember scattered details, like a couple of numbers and a great wall. I had no idea what the numbers or the wall meant, until my uncle came over one night and opened up a Bible. He asked me for the first number I remembered, and I told him *16.* He went to the sixteenth book of the Bible — the Book of Nehemiah. "What was the second number?" he asked, and I told him it was *6.* He went to the sixth chapter in Nehemiah and began reading it aloud.

It was all about how Nehemiah built a great wall.

Actually, Nehemiah restored the broken-down walls of Jerusalem. It was a job that should have taken years, but Nehemiah completely restored them and fortified Jerusalem in just fifty-two days. "When all our enemies heard about this, all the surrounding nations were afraid and lost their self-confidence," it says in Nehemiah 6:16, "because they realized that this work had been done with the help of our God."

At least now I knew what the wall in my dream meant, but I still didn't understand what it had to do with me. What kind of wall did God want me to restore? What was I supposed to do now? I kept thinking and praying about the wall, but I never got anywhere.

Then one day I came across a passage from the Book of Isaiah in a book I was reading.

"No longer will violence be heard in your land, nor ruin or destruction within your borders," it says in Isaiah 60:18, "but you will call your walls Salvation, and your gates Praise."

As I read it I realized that the wall in my dream had not been a literal wall. *The wall was God's salvation.* God had restored my ability to accept the salvation that Christ had died to give me, and now He was sending me out to tell others about it.

Now, I'm not in any way comparing myself to Nehemiah, not by a long shot. Even after everything I've experienced, I don't have all the answers or even most of the answers — I'm just an ordinary Christian who loves God dearly and is constantly searching for ways to get closer to Him. And my realization about what my dream meant did just that — it brought me closer to God.

You see, Christ died for my sins, but for much of my life I didn't believe that. I believed He died for *other* people's sins, just not mine. I believed I was too horrible, too undeserving of his compassion. And so I couldn't accept the salvation that Christ died to give me.

But then God gave me His wonderful gift, the gift of His glorious presence, and after that I *did* accept His salvation. I realized I wasn't undeserving or unforgiveable. God broke my cycle of pain and secrecy. God ripped away my curtain of shame. And now God wants me to share my story with others in the hopes that they, too, can accept His salvation. When I talk about all the things that happened in my life, I am hoping it empowers others to talk about their own lives, often for the very first time. And when they do, God breaks their cycles of pain and secrecy. God rips away their curtains of shame. And in this way their salvation is restored.

God's salvation was always there for them, as it was always there for me. God just needs us to accept it. He needs us to *choose* Him.

And that, I realized, is why God allowed me to think I'd be able to return to heaven, when all along His plan was to send me back. God gave me the *opportunity* to choose Him, and that's exactly what I did — I chose to stay with God. Before that I could

never fathom loving God more than anything else, but once I made the choice to
stay with Him I couldn't understand loving
anything more than God. God gave me that
choice so I would always remember choosing Him. The choice was everything.

But why, you might ask, was God's message delivered in such a confusing way? Why
did I have to have a dream, and then read
the Bible, and then read another book that
led me to the Isaiah verse? Why didn't God
just explain things to me clearly? It's because He needs us to *choose* Him. He
needs us to *want* to find Him. If God just
fed us instructions, we'd be nothing but
puppets. But God didn't create a world full
of puppets; He created living, breathing
people with free will. We don't choose God
because we have to. We choose God because
we want to.

I believe now that's why I witnessed those
demonic attacks. They've been the hardest
things for me to talk about and the events
that make me worry the most about sharing. But they happened, plain and simple,
and I've had to deal with them. They were
another step toward recognizing that God is
real. After all, if I was scared to death of
these demons — of the enemy — that meant
I had to believe the enemy was real. And if I

believed he was real, why wouldn't I believe God is real, too? The reason I was so vulnerable to the enemy was because of my fear. The enemy feeds on fear. I was like the lone sheep that strayed from the flock, forcing the shepherd to come find me. The enemy will go after you if you are alone and afraid. And I was alone, and I was deathly afraid . . . until I was saved.

Until God found me, and I found God.

Choosing that relationship with God is what salvation is all about. Salvation isn't some Get Out of Jail Free card that allows you to do anything you want and gives you a clean slate. The sins you commit on Earth will always have consequences. I still grieve for the child I lost when I was younger, and my heart still breaks whenever I think of all the bad decisions I made. My human form will always bear the scars of these sins, but because I chose God over everything else, God has cleansed my spirit. God has given me salvation. God has bathed me in His love.

Which is not to say that salvation is just reserving your spot in heaven. Salvation is something that exists *here on Earth.* God has a purpose for us here, today, right now. He wants us to live our lives in the kind of fullness and goodness that glorifies Him.

But we can't do that if we are plagued by secrets and shame. The walls of our salvation start to crumble and collapse, allowing the enemy to get in. And so we must make our walls Salvation, and our gates Praise. We must restore these walls, brick by brick, so that we can live in the fullness and glory of God.

The key, for me, was obedience. It took me a while to get there, but today when I hear God, I obey Him. I remember very clearly hearing God tell me that I would be writing this book. It was clear as day: *I am sending someone to help you tell your story.* And that's just what happened. Believe me, the hardest thing I've ever had to do was lay bare my life in these pages. It was painful to be so transparent, and I struggled with it mightily.

But that is what God wanted me to do, and so that is what I do. I go out and tell my story, and I share the message God sent me back to share. And what is that message? It is many things, but here is one way I would put it:

God is real, and we are all worthy of His love and salvation because He finds us worthy.

That may sound simple, but for me it changed everything. It was the answer I had spent so much time trying to find. And now that I have it, the fondest wish I have in my heart is for everyone — *everyone* — to have it, too. I want everyone to be there with me, in the bathing glow of God's love — even my worst enemy and the biggest sinners. It hurts me to think of *anyone* experiencing the opposite of what I experienced with God. No one should have to live in that horrible darkness.

And in the same way God forgave my sins, I no longer harbor anger or resentment toward anyone who has hurt me in my life. I love them deeply, and I hold them all close in my heart — my beautiful mother, who made mistakes but who never abandoned me, never stopped fighting for me; my father, who searched for love and acceptance just like I did, and who did the best he could to be my dad; my stepfather, who battled demons his whole life but who found ways to show a little girl love when he could; the people who abused me; the men who mistreated me; anyone I ever held a grudge against.

But most important, I have forgiven myself.

We are, all of us, God's perfect creations, and we are so worthy of His love.

CHAPTER NINETEEN

What happens now?

What comes next for me, now that I have died and gone to heaven and come back and shared God's message? What is the next stop on this amazing journey I'm on? I simply don't know — none of us knows what the future holds. But the beautiful part is, we don't need to. "For I know the plans I have for you," declares the Lord in Jeremiah 29:11, "plans to prosper you and not to harm you, plans to give you hope and a future."

These days I am grateful to God for so many things, but right up there at the top is my family. They give me such joy and happiness every day. Even Grandma Ernie, who I miss so much. I still think about hiding under her muumuu and walking around with her as she strolled through her lovely garden on these beautiful stepping-stones. I have those stones now, right in the front of my house. And every time I step on them, I miss my grandma. But I also know she's still with me, here in my heart.

I talk with my dad on the phone all the time, and we get along pretty well these days. I can talk to him about a lot of things I can't talk to my mom about, because she's likely to get all emotional, while my dad, who was never great at showing his emotions, always keeps an even keel. We're finding it easier and easier to be friends. The other day, I looked at Micah in his little glasses, and he looked so cute I scooped him up and gave him a big hug. As I hugged him I was struck by how much he looked like my dad in photos when he was that age. It made me wonder if my dad ever got scooped up and hugged like that when he was a kid. I took a picture and e-mailed it to my dad and told him I loved him. It was the closest thing to a hug I could give him.

I realize now he was a better father to me than I ever gave him credit for. And I know he loves me dearly. Those two years I spent with him in Illinois, he says now, were the two best years of his life.

And my mom . . . well, I just love my mom. Like I said, she's the only one who's been there for me my entire life, even when we fought like cats and dogs. I've never forgotten all her small acts of love and kindness, and I've even incorporated a couple of them — like the little notes on the napkins in my kids' lunchboxes — into my life. I learned a lot from my mother, and I still do.

The twins, thank God, are doing great. You watch them run around the living room chasing bubbles, and you'd never know they weighed less than a bag of sugar when they were born. I can't tell you how happy it makes me to see them with their father, who loves them like crazy. And what can I say about Virgil, the kindest and most loving man I've ever known? The way he supports me is so fierce and unending. God is my rock, that's for sure, but Virgil is my rock, too.

My son JP is growing up into a remarkable man. He is so loving and kind to his little brother and sisters, and his heart is always there for others who need it. He's a junior in high school now, and he plays the trumpet in the school band. He's also getting pretty good on the violin in his spare time. He doesn't remember much about the motorcycle accident, though he still has some pain in his knee on humid days and he can't hear at all out of his right ear. He constantly has to tell his friends, "Come around on my other side so I can hear you." There are days when he still feels angry, but he's worked so hard on being the best person he can be. His dream was to enlist in the military, but because of his hearing, he won't be able to do so. He's okay with it, though, because he has such a strong and personal relationship with God. "I see it as God redirecting my life so I can do what He wants me to do," he says. "I'm basically going with the flow. I'm throwing my lot in with God." Now his dream is to go to college and become a police officer, and I don't doubt he'll be a great one.

My beautiful daughter Sabyre, who's now a high school freshman, is really into music, too. She dreams of traveling to Nashville someday, and she loves Ed Sheeran and Taylor Swift and the band Jesus Culture. She hopes to record her own demo and maybe have a career as a singer. Let me tell you, she has a great voice, so I'm betting on her. She was even invited to join the praise and worship team at our church, which is a huge honor and accomplishment. I am so proud of her! Sabyre hasn't had much of a relationship with her biological father even though, God bless her, she's tried. Not too long ago she wrote a long heartfelt letter and sent it to her dad, who is now in prison, in the hopes they could at least talk once in a while. But he never wrote back. It broke my heart to see Sabyre checking the mailbox every day. But, like I said, kids are pretty resilient. Sabyre is determined to send her father a new letter *every week,* until he finally writes back.

And it will be in those letters that she fights for a father she cannot remember and ministers about a God he does not know. Like JP, Sabyre has a very strong relationship with God. Last summer she went away to a Christian youth camp, and the experience really affected her — so much so that Sabyre came to me and said, "Mom, I want to be baptized."

And so, on a very warm August day, we all drove out to Lake Altus, where everyone goes to swim and fish and lie on the beach. Sabyre asked Amber, who is like a big sister to her, to do the honors.

"Do you have a license to baptize me?" Sabyre joked with her.

"Oh, please," Amber said. Then she ran to her pastor and asked if she did indeed need a license to baptize someone. Turns out her love and passion for God was all the license required.

While JP watched the twins on shore, Sabyre, Virgil, Amber, and Brandon walked waist-deep into the water. I went in about knee deep so I could take pictures. Mind you, we were all still in our regular clothes, so we got a few funny looks from the other beachgoers. But, hey, I've learned that feeling embarrassed is a small price to pay to glorify God.

Amber got into the water carrying her grandfather's beat-up old blue King James Bible open to Colossians 2:13–14. As Brandon held Sabyre, Amber read from the Bible: "And you, being dead in your sins and the uncircumcision of your flesh, hath he quickened together with him, having forgiven you all trespasses; Blotting out the handwriting of ordinances that was against us, which was contrary to us, and took it out of the way, nailing it to his cross."

Then Brandon leaned Sabyre backward and dunked her in the water. Poor Sabyre hates fish for some reason, and she was terrified she'd feel some scaly thing brush up against her. She even joked she was bringing fish food so she could scatter it far away from where she was, but the fish stayed away. Sabyre came up from the cold water and Amber told her, "Go forward and live a new life of love and mercy, a life that glorifies God."

Afterwards, it was too hot to stick around

the lake for long, so we drove back home and had a Happy Baptism ice cream cake for Sabyre. The twins danced around like they always do, and everyone was happy and cheerful and feeling blessed. It was one of the best days of my life. I sat on my sofa, surrounded by my family, and I thought, *Thank you, God.*

Before all this happened I didn't know if God existed, and now I know — with more certainty than I know anything — that God is real.

Before all this I thought I wasn't worthy of His love and salvation, and now I know that I am.

Before all this I wondered what it was like to be in the presence of God, and now I know that it is glorious.

And that is something *all* of us can know.

You don't have to die and go to heaven. All you have to do to be in God's presence is choose Him.

All you have to do is *believe.*

It was only after I died and went to heaven that my mom dug through some of her old family albums and found this photo of me from when I was three years old. I'm wearing the same outfit I saw myself wearing in heaven.

"No, in all these things we are more than conquerors through him who loved us.
For I am convinced that neither death nor life,
nor angels nor demons, neither the present nor the future,
nor any powers, neither height nor depth,
nor anything else in all creation, will be able to separate us
from the love of God that is in Christ Jesus our Lord."

Romans 8:37–39

ACKNOWLEDGMENTS

CRYSTAL MCVEA

I'd like to thank the following people, without whom my story would not have been told.

Thank you to my husband, Virgil. Words can never express my love for you. You are the kindest, most honorable and loving man I've ever known. As our song says, "God blessed the broken road that led me straight to you." Thank you for being my best friend and the love of my life.

To my beautiful children, JP, Sabyre, Willow, and Micah — you four are the source of my greatest joy, love, and pride. Thank you for a lifetime of laughter and love.

To my parents — I love you both more than I've probably ever been able to convey. Thank you for loving me as I grew up and not killing me during my teenage years. I have a new appreciation for you both now that I am a parent. I wouldn't have chosen differently even if I could have.

To my brother, Jayson — you were my partner in crime and grew to be one of my dearest friends. Your constant encouragement and humor have kept me going through my life. You helped me to always laugh instead of cry. And for the record, you were *totally* worth my having to give away my dog. Melissa, thank you for loving my brother and completing his life. I love having you as my sister!

Kara Benton, you always believed in me and my story. Thank you for always cheering me on and just letting me be me!

Amber Taylor, you make me laugh like none other, and your faith and fire in God ignites me (and you, too, Brandon).

Patricia and Shearl, you inspire me so much; thank you for sharing your lives in this book.

Laura Schroff, thank you for being a ripple maker. Without you, my story would never have been told. What an invisible thread God weaved for you and me!

To all my friends and family — thank you for being my cheering section, a shoulder to cry on, and a source of powerful prayer warriors. Your love and encouragement mean more to me that you can ever know.

To the team at Howard Books, especially my wonderful editor, Jessica Wong, and Jonathan Merkh. Thank you so much for making the telling of my story possible. God placed an amazing team around me.

To Nena and Jan at Dupree-Miller — thank you for being the most amazing agents ever.

Last, but certainly not least, thank you, Alex Tresniowski. God promised me He was sending someone to tell my story, and you were well worth the wait. You have not only become my friend; you've become a part of my family forever.

ALEX TRESNIOWSKI

First, a giant thank-you to Crystal McVea for bringing me along on her amazing journey. I learned so much about courage and faith from you, and I feel so blessed to call you my friend. We'll be buddies forever. Thanks also to Virgil and your great kids, JP, Sabyre, Micah, and Willow for making me feel like a part of your beautiful family.

Thank you to my dear friend Laura Schroff, who changed my life and made this book possible. You're the most generous person I know. Thanks, everyone at Howard Books, especially my fellow introvert Jessica — you're brilliant. Thank you, Nena Madonia and Jan Miller — you're the best. Thanks to my golf buddy Mark Apovian, and thanks to J, for *Life of Pi.* Thanks to Fran, Rich, Zachary, Emily, Tam, Howie, Nick, Susan, and Humboldt for being the best family a guy could have. Thanks to Manley, Guy, LiLi, Nino, She She, and Ders for being my heart. Thanks to Amy, Neil, Siena, Karen, Greg, Ollie, Cutler, Jen, Kate, Angie, and Lindsay for making me feel so lucky.

And thank you, Lorraine Stundis, for everything.

WAKING UP IN HEAVEN
READING GROUP GUIDE

Waking Up in Heaven is the firsthand story of Crystal McVea and the day she died for nine minutes, went to heaven, and stood before God. In this remarkable autobiographical narrative, Crystal shares with readers her experience of walking with God toward the gates of heaven — a place so full of light and love that she did not want to return to Earth. But Crystal was revived — miraculously — and came back to consciousness in a hospital room with frantic doctors, nurses, and her own mother. Crystal's encounter with God made her a believer, despite her troubled, dark past. In *Waking Up in Heaven* Crystal shares her story — the good and the bad — in the hopes of spreading God's message of love and redemption.

DISCUSSION QUESTIONS

1. *Waking Up in Heaven* opens with a letter from Laura Schroff, author of *An Invisible Thread*. How does this letter help frame Crystal's story? What do you think made Laura pay attention to Crystal's message?

2. Revisit the moment when Crystal dies, beginning on page 32. What is your reaction to this scene? Are the details — the bright light, the warmth, the love — what you would expect? Why do you think Crystal chose to begin her story with her death, rather than with her troubled childhood?

3. Crystal describes the first person she met in heaven — herself: "Unlike on Earth, where I was plagued by doubts and fears, in heaven there was nothing but absolute certainty about who I was. . . . I was flooded with self-knowledge . . . revealing,

for the first time ever, the real me." Why do you think God reveals ourselves to us when we get to heaven? Do you think everyone on Earth is still waiting to meet himself or herself? What did Crystal learn about herself that surprised her? What do you imagine God might show you about yourself?

4. Crystal seems to have been followed by death for her entire life, beginning when her stepfather Hank "stood just inside [her] bedroom and aimed his gun at [her] bed." What are other moments in the story when Crystal comes face-to-face with death? What is the significance of so many close encounters?

5. "I was the common denominator. The problem had to lie with me," says Crystal, in reference to the abuse she endured from three different people during her childhood. Do you think Crystal's gut reaction to blame herself is typical? Describe a time in your life where a pattern of encounters has made you feel responsible, even though the situation may have been out of your control.

6. An important theme in Crystal's story is

forgiveness: forgiveness of herself, of her parents, of her abusers. Why is forgiveness so important to Crystal? Why was Crystal only able to find forgiveness in her heart *after* dying and meeting God?

7. How does suffering shape the person Crystal is today? In what ways has she suffered physically, mentally, economically, spiritually? Have you had similar struggles in your life? Do you believe like Crystal that "suffering can bring us even closer to Him" and that "our very worst moments are precisely when God's grace is most brightly revealed"? Why or why not?

8. Discuss Virgil. What role does he play in "saving" Crystal's life? How would you characterize him? Do you see him as angel-like? Crystal says that Virgil brought stability to her life, but what else did he bring?

9. Crystal talks about her demonic events as tests from God to strengthen her faith. How would you describe these events?

10. What are the ways in which Crystal describes God making her feel "whole" (259), and why is this feeling so

important?

11. What does Crystal see as her mission from God? What made her realize this mission? Who do you think you are called to be?

12. Crystal defines God's message as the following: "God is real, and we are all worthy of His love and salvation because He finds us worthy." Crystal understands God's role as a parent who loves His children. Do you think of God as a parent figure? If you had to define God's message to you, what would it be?

13. Do you think that Crystal's story of dying and coming back to life is important for us to hear? In what ways? What does *Waking Up in Heaven* teach us about blind faith?

ADDITIONAL ACTIVITIES: WAYS OF ENHANCING YOUR BOOK CLUB

1. In *Waking Up in Heaven,* Crystal quotes scripture frequently in order to explain God's plan at work in her life. Read the passage from Romans 8:37–39 aloud to your group:

No, in all these things we are more than conquerors through him who loved us. For I am convinced that neither death nor life, nor angels nor demons, neither the present nor the future, nor any powers, neither height nor depth, nor anything else in all creation, will be able to separate us from the love of God that is in Christ Jesus our Lord.

Why do you think Crystal chose to conclude her story with this passage? How do you think this passage acts as a synopsis of the narrative? Is there anything in your life that has tried to separate you from God's love?

How did you overcome this separation and regain your faith? Share with your group favorite scripture passages that have helped you endure tests of faith or separation from God.

2. Crystal speaks of the beauty of her home state of Oklahoma, land that is "broad and flat and beautiful." She references the Native American poet N. Scott Momaday, who wrote about the beauty of this land that surely "is where creation was begun" (173). With your group, read the poem "The Delight Song of Tsoai-talee" by N. Scott Momaday from The Poetry Foundation: http://www.poetryfoundation.org/poem/175895. How does this poem speak to Crystal's message that God loves us and that our lives are valuable in His eyes? What line of this poem speaks most to you? Why?

3. From God's "nudges" Crystal has had the opportunity to meet many people from all walks of life. These "nudges" have even led Crystal down roads that she might never have traveled otherwise. One such "nudge" came to Crystal while watching *Dr. Phil.* Writing to Laura Schroff led to the creation of *Waking Up in Heaven.* Read

Laura's book *An Invisible Thread* with your reading group. Why do you think God "nudged" Crystal to contact Laura? What is the connection between their two stories? How does God's love manifest itself in Laura's narrative? In Crystal's? In yours?

QUESTIONS FOR
CRYSTAL McVEA

You say that your last direct communication from God was the most powerful because He told you: "Tell them what you can remember." Why was this the most powerful and important communication from God? Why do you think God asked you to share your story?

When God said, "Tell them what you can remember," He was telling me what He wanted me to do with the rest of my life. And that is a very, very powerful thing to hear directly from God. This is why He sent me back, why I'm here today and not in heaven. It's because God still has a plan for me on Earth. And I understand now that the reason He wants me to share my life story is because of all the other people out there who are going through the same struggles and facing the same challenges as I did. God is sending them the mes-

sage that He is real and He loves them and they are worthy of His love, just as He communicated that message to me. And I think the story of my time in heaven by itself wouldn't be as powerful without the story of my life and who I was before I met God.

In *Waking Up in Heaven,* you alternate between your encounter with God and the story of your life, past and present. Why did you decide to structure your story this way? Do you think that the non-linear format reflects God's way of communicating with us?

The truth is that God has been in my life and all over my life forever, and I just wasn't aware of it. It's like those dreams that He gave me and that I didn't understand, and it was only many years later that I was able to look back and figure out they were God's way of telling me something. So for me, having the heaven chapters appear throughout the book is a way of reinforcing that God was always there for me, that there was never a period of my life when He wasn't there. God was always a presence in my life, except I didn't always notice Him. And my time in heaven allowed me to look back on my life with a new perspec-

tive and realize He was always there. And I wanted the book to have that same feeling — that God is always there, always trying to communicate with us, even in the worst and hardest times of our lives.

When you talk about "the enemy," are you referring to the Devil or some other form of evil? How can we recognize "the enemy" in your estimation?

When I say "the enemy," I mean Satan and the demonic realm. In John 10 and many other scriptures, Jesus warns us about the enemy. So many times people believe in God but not in the enemy that Jesus tells us about. One of my favorite quotes says, "The greatest trick the Devil ever pulled off was making the world believe he didn't exist." Imagine the havoc that the enemy can wreak in your life if you don't even believe he is real. I think we can recognize the work of Satan or demons by simply listening to the warning of Jesus — that the enemy comes to kill, steal, and destroy.

You describe the many women who have shared their stories of struggle and

heartbreak after hearing your testimony. Do you find that your story is especially important for women who have endured abuse? Do you feel particularly called to empower women?

It's true that a lot of women have come up to me and shared their stories, but I believe my testimony is aimed at anyone who is searching for God, men and women alike. The things I went through — the abortion, the sexual abuse, abandonment — those are things that don't only affect women. Abortions affect men, too. Sexual abuse affects everyone. Now, my story may be especially relevant to women, because it is told through a woman's perspective, and women can relate to the things I discuss. But I truly believe my testimony is relevant to anyone and everyone who wants to know, "Is God real? Does He love me? Do I matter?" Finding the answers to these questions can empower everyone, men and women alike.

Talk more about the "nudges" that God gives to you. How can you tell the difference between your voice and God's?

When God tells me to do something, it's usually something I don't want to do and/or feel embarrassed about doing. It's like the day I watched Dr. Phil *and saw Laura Schroff on the show, and God nudged me to contact her about helping me with my book. And I just didn't want to do it. I didn't want to contact this complete stranger and tell her my whole story, and I prayed and prayed not to have to do it, but God kept nudging me, and finally I did it. And it worked out. Or the time God nudged me to give the waitress a $100 tip. That is the last thing I wanted to do, because I just didn't have the money. But the beauty of God's nudges is that He usually shows me why He wanted me to do something once I've finally done it. And I can tell the difference between God's voice and my own voice because my own voice second-guesses everything. But God's voice is firm.*

Do you think the first step to believing in God's love is forgiveness? Was that the first step you had to take in order to become a believer?

Actually, for me the very first step toward believing in God's love was beginning a relationship with Jesus Christ. I just started talking to him. I asked him to come into my life and my heart. I was plagued with doubt my entire life. But even when I wasn't sure, I always kept talking to Jesus and God. From the time I was a kid to when I died, I was always asking God questions and asking Him to prove things to me. My heart was open to the possibility that God is real and that He loves me, even if my brain wasn't. For me, the ability to forgive came later.

If you had to name a theme of your story, what would it be and why?

Oh gosh, I don't know. I just think my life is like everybody else's, and that all of our lives are an endless pursuit of God. And God never stops pursuing us, no matter how far we stray, no matter how far we fall. So I guess the theme could be that God's love never fails us. It never fails. And once we realize that, it changes everything. So my story is about my pursuit of God, and God's pursuit of me. The thing is, I have always seen my story as a beautiful love story. It's a story about all the amazing things He has done for me on this journey. It's a love story about God's love for me, and for all of us.

What has been the most challenging

aspect of sharing your story of meeting God? What has been the most rewarding?

The challenging part was having to open up every part of my life to the world, which I really did not want to do. Being so transparent, so open about every aspect of my life, was very, very hard. But God told me to tell them everything, and that's just what I did. And the most rewarding thing has been watching what God is doing with my testimony in other people's lives. I get to be a witness to this awesome thing that is happening because of God's amazing grace, and because of what God has done for me. Look, I am not the greatest public speaker, and in fact I really dislike speaking in front of large groups. But when people tell me what God has done for them in their lives because of my story, it makes it all worth it a hundred times over.

What advice do you give to readers who struggle with their faith?

Usually when I talk to someone who is struggling I say, "Listen, you could not be any more skeptical than I was. Believe me, I've been there." And then I tell them that no matter what they have to keep the faith that God is real.

They can never stop pursuing Him, never stop trying to find Him, never stop talking to Him. Do not close that line of communication. Do not shut Him out. It's the same as the relationships in our lives — you can't have a relationship without communication. You have to keep the lines open. Today I talk to God all the time. When I'm vacuuming or doing the dishes or driving, whatever. And it's not always good stuff. Sometimes I say, "God, today really sucks." But if you're struggling with your faith, you have to keep trying and talking and searching, and God will find you.

Describe the process of writing this book. Did God "nudge" you in any particular direction? Do you believe that God called you to share this story with the world?

The process of making this book happen could be a book all its own. It was full of twists and turns and crazy events. And even when things fell into place and the book started to become real, all I ever heard was, "This usually doesn't happen. Books don't usually happen this way." So I know it was God's hand at work. It was God who steered me to Laura Schroff, who steered me to my cowriter, Alex

Tresniowski, who steered me to Howard Books. And the process itself was hard some-times, and there were days when I wondered if God had made a mistake by choosing me, but in the end it all worked out. So yes, I absolutely believe that God wanted me to share my story, and steered me toward the right people, and that is why I couldn't stay with Him in heaven. Because His plan for me on Earth isn't finished.

What lesson do you hope that readers will take away from this story?

So many people do not realize that God loves them and that they are worthy of His love. So the lesson is, no matter what you've done or who you are, you are worthy because God loves you. You matter as a person because you are God's child. All of us, every single one of us, even those who don't believe in Him — He just loves us and finds us worthy of that love. That isn't always an easy thing to understand or accept. The story of my life cov-ers a lot of different sins, including a sin I believed was too horrible to ever be forgiven. But even with all that, God found me worthy of His love, and kept pursuing me. God pursues everyone. He wants the people who abused me just as much as He wants me. He is in an endless pursuit of their lives and hearts. So I hope that people read my story and believe that God's love is so vast and so powerful and so encompassing, and that they have a place alongside Him, in the splendor of His love.

The employees of Thorndike Press hope you have enjoyed this Large Print book. All our Thorndike, Wheeler, and Kennebec Large Print titles are designed for easy reading, and all our books are made to last. Other Thorndike Press Large Print books are available at your library, through selected bookstores, or directly from us.

For information about titles, please call:
(800) 223-1244

or visit our Web site at:
http://gale.cengage.com/thorndike

To share your comments, please write:
Publisher
Thorndike Press
10 Water St., Suite 310
Waterville, ME 04901